The Arab Gulf States

THE WASHINGTON PAPERS

... intended to meet the need for an authoritative, yet prompt, public appraisal of the major developments in world affairs.

President, CSIS: Amos A. Jordan

Series Editor: Walter Laqueur

Director of Publications: Nancy B. Eddy

Managing Editor: Donna R. Spitler

MANUSCRIPT SUBMISSION

The Washington Papers and Praeger Publishers welcome inquiries concerning manuscript submissions. Please include with your inquiry a curriculum vitae, synopsis, table of contents, and estimated manuscript length. Manuscripts must be between 120–200 double-spaced typed pages. All submissions will be peer reviewed. Submissions to *The Washington Papers* should be sent to *The Washington Papers*; The Center for Strategic and International Studies; 1800 K Street NW; Suite 400; Washington, DC 20006. Book proposals should be sent to Praeger Publishers; One Madison Avenue; New York NY 10010.

The Arab Gulf States

Steps Toward Political Participation

J. E. Peterson

Foreword by Majid Khadduri

Published with The Center for
Strategic and International Studies
Washington, D.C.

PRAEGER

New York
Westport, Connecticut
London

Library of Congress Cataloging-in-Publication Data

Peterson, John E., 1947–
  The Arab gulf states : steps toward political participation / J. E.
Peterson.
      p. cm. – (Washington papers, ISSN 0278-937x : 131)
  "Published with the Center for Strategic and International Studies,
Washington, D.C."
  Includes index.
  ISBN 0-275-92881-0 (alk. paper). ISBN 0-275-92882-9 (pbk. : alk.
paper)
  1. Representative government and representation – Persian Gulf
States. 2. Political participation – Persian Gulf States. 3. Legislative
bodies – Persian Gulf States. 4. Persian Gulf States – Politics and
government. I. Center for Strategic and International
Studies. II. Title.
JQ1825.P459P48 1987
323'.042'09536 – dc19   87-25836

Library of Congress Catalog Card Number: 87-25836
ISBN: 0-275-92881-0 (cloth)
        0-275-92882-9 (paper)

First published in 1988

Praeger Publishers, One Madison Avenue, New York, NY 10010
A division of Greenwood Press, Inc.

Printed in the United States of America

∞

The paper used in this book complies with the Permanent
Paper Standard issued by the National Information Standards
Organization (Z39.48-1984).

10 9 8 7 6 5 4 3 2 1

Contents

Foreword

In recent years a number of studies on the political structure of the Gulf states has been published, each a case study on a single Gulf country. It is, indeed, gratifying to note the increasing number of writers who have taken an interest in Gulf affairs and provide us not only with general information but often with insight into the structure of society, the political processes, and the character of the *dramatis personae* involved in them.

The case method is, of course, very important; but it is not enough for an overall picture of Arabian politics. Most Gulf writers seem to have paid little or no attention to a broader understanding of the subject. Indeed, there is at this juncture a need for a comparative study of Arabian politics and its underlying social forces that would correlate and sum up the findings of researchers. In his work on political participation in the Arab Gulf States, Dr. J. E. Peterson has pioneered in exploring the role of "national councils" as a form of political participation in the six Arab Gulf countries. He has not only reconstructed from information now available to us a synthesis of the modes of political participation through "national councils," but also has analyzed how the regime and the leadership of each country has rationalized, if not legitimized, the establishment of national councils. But his study, I hasten to add, is based on much more than the material already in print; he is, in his own right, the author of more than one case study, and he has drawn on his own observations and experiences during many extended research visits to almost all the Arab Gulf countries.

In his study of political participation, however, J. E. Peterson has dealt with only six countries; two – North and South Yemen – have been excluded. He has perhaps good reason to exclude South Yemen, owing to the absence of political participation under a Marxist regime. But in North Yemen, political participation through a national council is considered an integral part of the political system, even though the whole regime was established by a military coup to replace an older regime based on Islamic and tribal traditions. Since the two Yemens have chosen the course of political development through revolutionary coups – a method unacceptable to the six members of the Arab Gulf Cooperation Council (GCC) – Peterson has decided to exclude them from his work. Because of their location in Arabia, however, the GCC members have not given up the hope that, by extending economic assistance, they might eventually alter their neighbors' course of political development. It is hoped that a second edition of this study might include political participation in the two Yemens.

Two fundamental traditions – Islam and tribalism – have been rightly suggested by Peterson as a possible rationalization for the establishment of national councils in the Arab Gulf countries. The Islamic principle of consultation (*shura*) prescribes that rulers should "consult" notables (presumably on behalf of the people) on all matters of public concern (*Qu'ran XXII*, 32; *XL*, 36). Following World War I, the modernists in northern Arab countries construed these divine injunctions as a license to adopt a Western style of parliamentary democracy. Later, however, when this type of political participation was dominated by authoritarian rulers and vested interests, it was discredited and replaced by military dictatorships on the ground that it did not measure up to expectations. These unhappy experiences exacted a high price at the expense of individual liberty and taught other Islamic lands to avoid the verdict that history repeats itself.

When foreign influence began to recede from Arab Gulf dependencies and their income from oil became available for development, the rulers of those countries had reason to believe that the Islamic principle of consultation did not necessarily call for the adoption of a Western style of parliamentary democracy. Rather than follow in the footsteps of northern Arab neighbors and face the likely social upheavals and military coups, the ruling dynasties of Arabia sought to adopt a conservative interpretation of the principle of consultation. They decided to establish national councils, some elected and others appointed (but not necessarily unrepresentative), with limited powers to exercise political particpation in such matters as legislation and other discretionary functions.

Peterson has taken pains to describe in detail the structure and functions of the councils and the extent to which each national council has been allowed to participate in the regime of each Gulf country. In Saudi Arabia, where a national council has not yet been established but is still pledged in principle, Peterson has indicated that some other forms of "consultation" have been pursued according to tribal traditions. The king and his principal deputy premiers are available, for example, to "sit in Council (*majlis*)" with tribal shaykhs and other notables to discuss complaints, problems, and other matters.

But Islam is not the only source of political participation in the Gulf countries. Arab tribal tradition also requires the chief (shaykh) of each tribe to consult notables and senior members of the tribe about their affairs; the paramount chief of a tribal confederation is also bound to consult the shaykhs of all the tribes of the confederation on their affairs. Without consultation, no allegiance is owed to a chief who does not "sit in *majlis*" with the notables and senior members of the tribe to exchange views on all matters of public concern. This rapport between chief and tribe, created through the instrumentality of the *majlis*, has been finely expressed in the parable of the "tent" in an ode by Abu Tammam (d.850) in his diwan *al-Hamasa*:

> A folk that hath no chiefs must soon decay,
> And chiefs it hath not when the vulgar sway.
> Only with poles the tent is reared at last,
> But when the pegs and poles are once combined,
> Then stand accomplished that which was designed.

The tribal chief, though only a *primus inter pares* in principle, undertakes the authority entrusted into his hands very seriously. Since he is solely responsible for the security and welfare of the tribe, he is bound to listen to all conflicting views and opinions, but final decision is always left up to him, presumably on the ground that his judgment is guided by wisdom and experience. But if he is often faulted, he is likely to be replaced by another enjoying higher prestige and a reputation for good judgment.

Today all the Gulf states are presided over by tribal rulers. Since all profess Islam, they have sought to legitimize their political systems on the grounds of both Islamic and tribal traditions. J. E. Peterson, however, is not unaware that tribal traditions have often been used to justify authoritarian propensities. They have also served to strike a balance between the high expectations of the new generation and the pressure created by religious groups that demand the enforcement of Islamic law without regard for the new conditions and ideas resulting from the income of oil.

Majid Khadduri
School of Advanced International Studies
The Johns Hopkins University

About the Author

J. E. Peterson is a writer and consultant on contemporary Middle Eastern affairs and also is an adjunct fellow in Middle East studies at the Center for Strategic and International Studies. He received his B.A. and M.A. degrees from the University of Arizona and his Ph.D. from the School of Advanced International Studies (SAIS) of The Johns Hopkins University.

Dr. Peterson has been a research analyst for the Library of Congress and has taught at Bowdoin College, the College of William and Mary, the University of Pennsylvania, and Portland State University. He has also served as a research fellow at the Middle East Institute and adjunct scholar at the Foreign Policy Research Institute. He has conducted extensive research in the Middle East and has been the recipient of fellowships and grants from the Shell Foundation, the Social Science Research Council, the Earhart Foundation, and the Fulbright program. During 1983 and 1984, he served as the Thornton D. Hooper fellow in international security affairs at the Foreign Policy Research Institute of Philadelphia.

Among his publications are *The Sultanate of Oman and Emirates of Eastern Arabia* (coauthor, 1976), *Oman in the Twentieth Century* (1978), *Conflict in the Yemens and Su-*

perpower Involvement (1981), *Yemen: The Search for a Modern State* (1982), *The Politics of Middle Eastern Oil* (ed., 1983), and *Security in the Arabian Peninsula and Gulf States* (1985). His latest book, *Defending Arabia*, was published by Croom Helm (London) and St. Martin's Press (New York) in 1986.

Acknowledgments

Research for this study during 1985 and 1986 in all six states of the Gulf Cooperation Council was assisted by a Senior Research Grant in the Fulbright Islamic Civilization Research Program, and further archival research in London in 1987 was made possible by an American Political Science Association Research Grant. I would like to thank Professor Dale F. Eickelman of New York University, Professor James P. Piscatori of the School of Advanced International Studies (SAIS) of The Johns Hopkins University, and former Ambassador Sadek J. Sulaiman of Oman for their invaluable comments on earlier drafts and Steven R. Dorr for his comments on Qatar. Naturally, all responsibility for errors of fact and interpretation is mine alone.

The Arab Gulf States

1

Political Change and Participation in the Gulf Cooperation Council States

For decades, the imminent demise of the monarchies of the Gulf has been predicted. They have been described facilely as anachronistic absolute monarchies in an age of republics and democratic aspirations. But the Gulf monarchies – Saudi Arabia, Kuwait, Bahrain, Qatar, the United Arab Emirates (UAE), and Oman – have confounded their critics, surviving both the challenge of the radical Left and, so far, that of the Islamic Right. Far from being fragile crumbling relics from the past, these young states have confronted the challenge of development and, in many respects, have matured and grown even stronger.

The rapid enhancement of the rulers' powers, shared – often tensely – with close relatives at the onset of the oil era, has been superseded by a gradual diffusion of that power to state institutions. The role and capabilities of the state have expanded tremendously, and the state increasingly has enhanced its political power. The influence of members of the ruling families on state policy meanwhile has declined in a relative sense, although not as sharply as has the influence of other notable families, especially among the merchant houses, religious leadership, and allied tribes. As the machinery and institutions of the state have become

more accepted, entrenched, and complex, political participation and representation necessarily have become more
formal. Thus the need for national councils – representative
assemblies or consultative councils with either elected or
appointed members.

This study is an examination of political participation
in these six monarchies, all member states of the Gulf Cooperation Council (GCC), concentrating on the background to
popular demands for representation and the regimes' establishment of national councils. Five of the six states have
established a national council at some point (see table 1).
The existing bodies remain consultative councils, while the
two elected councils have been suspended. This inevitably
raises questions about the suitability of such formal bodies
in these largely traditional societies, the commitment of the
regimes to formal participation, given the suspension of the
elected assemblies and lack of tolerance for "loyal opposition" and dissent, and the functions of existing consultative
councils: Do they represent the people or do they merely
serve as organs of the state?

Rather than static entities, increasingly anachronistic,
the Arab Gulf states are better described as newly emergent post-traditional states. Compared to other Arab and
Third World states, they are well able to provide for the
needs of their citizenry, and the few short decades of oil-
fueled modernization have been accompanied by a significant degree of political development, albeit in narrowly
channeled directions. The extent of such development appears to be largely dependent on the length of time the
modern states have had to solidify and evolve.

Political change has occurred in several stages. With
the discovery of oil and the accumulation of oil wealth came
an aggregation of power by the ruler and the ruling family.
Oil income was seen as a fief for the benefit of the ruling
family, either directly through the provision of generous
allowances or indirectly through manipulation of nascent
government agencies letting development contracts. Only

gradually was the ruler, and thereby the state, able to reassert control of the purse and of government organs.

After a decade or so, a new phase, "constitutionalization," was instituted. This generally involved the adoption of a written constitution at independence, with some attempt at transference of the right to rule from simply tradition, within a tribal and Islamic context, to the exercise of authority in the name of the people, with whom sovereignty theoretically rests. In theory, members of the ruling families are under the same obligations and constraints as are all citizens, although this remains subject to abuse, and the ruling families continue to monopolize power. The rest of the citizenry will tolerate this monopoly only as long as it continues to perceive the monarchical system as legitimate and accepts the authority of these ruling families.

The primary objective of all these states has been to promote wide-ranging economic development while simultaneously attempting to preserve the traditional nature of society and, by implication, the traditional political structure. Essentially, the Arab Gulf states are capitalist societies, in which ruling families govern on the basis of a combination of traditional right and an adherence to an equitable allocation of the benefits of oil wealth and concomitant economic opportunities. For the most part, social distinctions in the Arab Gulf are not made on the basis of economic class or standing but are hereditary.[1] Economic mobility, however, is prevalent and accepted – and was not difficult to achieve during the halcyon days of the oil era.

One of the most durable and far-reaching effects during this period of political change has been the process of institutionalization, which has embraced a number of aspects. There has been an emphasis on constitutionalism, both in the writing of formal constitutions and in the creation of a broader constitutional framework, which defines the nature and organization of the state and determines the scope and extent of activities of the regime. Second, the government structure has expanded tremendously as a result of a

TABLE 1
The Member States of the Gulf Cooperation Council

Country	Ruler	Ruling Family	Total Population (m)	Citizen Population[1]	National Council
Bahrain	'Isa ibn Salman (Amir)	Al Khalifa	0.41	66%	National Assembly (1973–1975)
Kuwait	Jabir al-Ahmad (Amir)	Al Sabah	1.70	40%	National Assembly (1962–1976, 1981–1986)
Qatar	Khalifa ibn Hamad (Amir)	Al Thani	0.27	25%	Advisory Council
Oman	Qabus ibn Sa'id (Sultan)	Al Bu Sa'id	1.30	78%	State Consultative Council

Saudi Arabia	Fahd ibn 'Abd al-'Aziz (King)	Al Sa'ud	11.00	60%	—
United Arab Emirates	Zayid ibn Sultan[2] (President)	—[3]	1.60	20%	Federal National Council; National Consultative Council[4]

Notes:

1. Population figures are author's estimates, extrapolating from recent editions of each country's statistical yearbook or other sources.

2. Shaykh Zayid, the ruler of Abu Dhabi, has served as the only president of the seven-member United Arab Emirates (UAE) since independence in 1971 and was elected by his fellow rulers to a fourth five-year term in 1986. Similarly, Shaykh Rashid ibn Sa'id, the ruler of Dubai, has served as the UAE's only vice president.

3. There is a separate ruling family for each of the seven component states of the UAE. Abu Dhabi's Shaykh Zayid belongs to the Al Nahyan, while Dubai's Shaykh Rashid is from the Al Maktum.

4. Serves the amirate of Abu Dhabi only.

change in expectations – from a government that plays a minimalist role and exercises a few limited functions, to a government that is the source of nearly all authority and prosperity. Third, the rough-and-ready justice, based on Islamic and customary precepts dispensed by rulers in the past, has given way to a complex legal structure, partly Islamic, partly Western, and embracing commercial, banking, labor, traffic, administrative, and criminal regulations.[2]

Changing Requirements for Legitimacy

Three broadly defined phases of political change can be discerned in the Arabian Peninsula: the traditional, the neotraditional, and the modernizing or post-traditional.[3] Decentralization and limited central authority characterized the political systems of the traditional phase, and the exercise of power conformed to the goals, responsibilities, and constraints long present in traditional, inward-looking societies. The neotraditional phase occurring in Yemen and Oman produced political systems based on the personal strength of a single individual introducing certain significant innovations into the system – particularly as they enhanced his own authority – in a defensive and ultimately futile attempt to maintain the traditional nature of the society. The modernizing phase was initiated by radical policies of socioeconomic development, including the necessary restructuring of replacement of regimes and a redefinition or expansion of the scope and role of the state.

Apart from Oman, the neotraditional phase in the Arab Gulf states was limited geographically to only a few instances and, in time, to the early years of the oil era. Abu Dhabi's Shaykh Shakhbut is perhaps the best-known example of a neotraditional ruler: refusing to spend the amirate's new oil income, he was deposed with British assistance in 1968 and replaced by his brother Zayid. More generally, however, the Gulf states moved directly from a traditional stage to a post-traditional stage, albeit with strong traditionalist influences.[4] The official adoption of the post-traditional or modernizing course of action, of course, is clearly distinct from the actual establishment of an environment conducive to its accomplishment.

In recent decades, the impact of socioeconomic development and the process of institutionalization have necessitated a reformulation of the basis of legitimacy. There was no uncertainty about "legitimacy" prior to the early twentieth century. The right to rule belonged to whoever possessed the historical claim to leadership, had the physical power to dominate in society (and within ruling families), and could control the available natural resources. With the introduction of administrative reforms, new sources of "legitimacy" emerged: a corpus of laws, announcements, decisions, or decrees made and enacted by increasingly sophisticated governments, followed intermittently by a system of representation in municipal councils, education, or health committees. Following independence in Kuwait and Bahrain, national assemblies were created to give regimes an aura of "legitimacy" through public delegation.[5] No longer could traditional criteria be the sole determinants of legitimacy. Increasingly, regimes and ruling families must base their right to rule on a fusion of traditional and new "rationalist" elements.

The regimes' conception of governance was described by a senior member of Saudi Arabia's ruling family in the following words:

> The regime in the Saudi Arabian Kingdom is Islamic, stemming from the Islamic law which is the constitution of the Saudi state. It is what determines the relationship between the ruler and the ruled and it is what settles all matters pertaining to the citizens and residents here. Naturally there is a need, indeed it is essential to tidy up this relationship. This is done through systems decided upon by the legislative and executive arms which are embodied in royal edicts. They are based on the tolerant Islamic spirit and on Islamic values, and on the Arab heritage which the Saudi Arabian Kingdom upholds.

From here comes the genuine cohesion between the ruler and the ruled and the continuing dialogue between them. The state and its leaders believe that direct contact is better and more successful. Hence the doors are open before the citizens to contact the officials headed by the king of the country, his crown prince, and all the other officials so that those in positions of responsibility will be familiar with what interests the citizens and their aspirations. . . . [Saudi Arabia] feels that it has a major mission to perform — to prove to the whole world that it is possible, indeed, it is one of the facts of life that an Islamic state should take its place in this age although, unfortunately, we find some rejection of it even by some Muslims, a matter which pains us.[6]

The traditional pillars of the ruling families' legitimacy were based on reference to an idealized notion of traditional power-sharing in tribal society and Islam as represented in the *shari'a* (Islamic law). Historically, the leader of the tribal community essentially served as a *primus inter pares*, a "chairman" rather than a ruler, who consulted tribal, religious, and merchant notables of the community before taking action. This allusion is reflected in the use of the term *mubaya'a* (pledge of allegiance) in the National Assembly's approval of new heirs apparent. Rulers also found it necessary to govern in accordance with, or at least in reference to, the Islamic principles of *shura* (consultation) and *ijma'* (consensus). The Islamic basis of *shura* rests on the Quranic verse in the *sura* (chapter) of the same name, "whose affairs are conducted by mutual consultation" (*wa-amruhum shura baynahum*, Sura 42, v. 38), which "suggests the ideal way in which a good man should conduct his affairs" and, by implication, the way in which the state should conduct its affairs.[7] Reference is also made to the verse, "and consult with them in affairs" (*wa-shawaruhum fil-amr*, Sura 3, v. 159).[8] Amir Jabir of Kuwait reaffirmed the central importance of this principle in 1986 when he asserted that we have all put our faith in *shura*, which was passed on to us from the book of our God, when he said "Their affairs to be counselled among themselves," and his word, "You have consulted on the affair." We practiced this consultation at the levels of the family, neighbors, and relatives, and the homeland.[9]

To these traditional pillars of legitimacy, the newly emergent states of the Gulf have added policies of distributing material benefits to nearly all sectors of the citizenry, rationalist constitutional frameworks, newly institutionalized government structures generally responsive to popular demands, and military-security apparatuses capable of controlling the population. The four written constitutions in Kuwait, Bahrain, Qatar, and the UAE place emphasis on Western-inspired principles of sovereignty residing in the people, the separation of powers between the branches of government, and some degree of legislative power-sharing between the ruler and national councils, in addition to Islamic precepts. Saudi Arabia maintains that the *shari'a* provides its constitution, while the constitutional framework of Oman is implied.

The attempt to marry traditional and rationalist bases of legitimacy is not without its dangers. References to Islamic justifications of rule pose perils because divergences from strict interpretations open regimes to charges that they are introducing *bid'a* (innovation) and are therefore un-Islamic. Constitutional provisions declaring that sovereighty lies in the people runs counter to accepted interpretations that political sovereignty in Islam belongs to God.

Another dilemma arises from the naming of national councils. On the surface, *majlis al-shura* is the logical choice. *Majlis* represents the form of the institution and *shura* its constitutional essence. Despite the very great differences between the recent national councils of Kuwait and Bahrain and those of Qatar, the UAE, and Oman, all five have used *majlis* in their titles. *Majlis* is susceptible to a wide variety of meanings, depending on context, including place (as in a meeting room), group (a social gathering), or an institution (committee, board, or court). It is widely used for parliament throughout the Islamic world. Although this was the intention in Kuwait and Bahrain, the intended connotation in the other three states is apparently closer to committee or commission, with subreference to the traditional informal *majlis* with its atmosphere of a relatively free exchange of ideas and opinions on a wide variety of social, economic, and political matters.

But *shura* is a troublesome concept for regimes to employ because it evokes the golden age of the Rashidun caliphs, the first four successors to the Prophet Muhammad. Abu Bakr, the first caliph, informally consulted a few advisers on the choice of his successor, and 'Umar, the second caliph, appointed a *majlis al-shura* before his death, which decided on 'Uthman as his successor.[10] *Shura* therefore reflects an ideal of full interchange between ruler and ruled that is absent from the modern Islamic world. More specifically, it has been widely interpreted in the last century as justifying or requiring representative government, beginning with the insistence of Islamic reformer Jamal al-Din al-Afghani (1838–1897) that "authority ultimately belongs to the people and rulers have no right to govern without the consent of their subjects."[11] As a consequence, there is a tendency to use other names for parliamentary bodies.[12]

In another illustration of potential pitfalls, Kuwait's decision to set the voting age at 21 and Bahrain's to choose 20 (Qatar's electorate would have been at least 24) theoretically opens them to the charge that they are un-Islamic, because the traditional Islamic interpretation holds that there is no specific age when children become mature; maturity comes at different times for each individual. The Islamic Republic of Iran found it necessary to grapple with this issue when drawing up regulations for its *majlis*. Eventually, drawing on Islamic precedent, it was decided to make 16-year-olds eligible to vote, giving Iran one of the youngest voting ages anywhere.

But traditionalist objections need not be based solely on Islamic precepts. The Gulf states are no longer traditional tribal societies, and ruling families increasingly risk being perceived as an elitist class acting solely in their own interests rather than those of the state or the population as a whole. Attempts to retain symbols of traditional legitimacy may go awry. In Oman, the sultan periodically engages in grand tours of the country's interior, stopping in selected villages for highly ceremonial *majlis*es with the local population. He is accompanied by his council of ministers, all of whom must carry rifles. Because security is handled by proper guards, the arming of these officials obviously is symbolic and apparently is meant to represent the authority of the state. But it also has the effect of dividing those present at such gatherings into rulers, who possess strength and power (*shadid*), and the ruled, who are unarmed and weak or inferior (*da'if*).

Appeals to newer foundations of legitimacy are necessary, but also are fraught with drawbacks. Ruling families have sought to bolster their position by actively pursuing widespread distributive policies. They have also encouraged informal participation through both traditional means (such as the *majlis*) and new institutions (the formal national councils), as long as such participation is limited to the expression of material needs and concerns and is not overtly critical of the system and the ruling families. The more regimes seek to present themselves as legitimate on newer lines and sponsor socioeconomic change, the more they lose credibility with the traditionalist elements of society and expose themselves to charges that they are un-Islamic. This appeared to be less a danger during the 1950s and 1960s, when the formation of state structures in the Gulf was influenced by an atmosphere of secular pan-Arabist and socialist ideologies, than in the 1980s.

The younger generation has grown up perceiving the state as the source of everything. They are overwhelmingly dependent on the state for jobs, and even for those in private business the state is the ultimate source of income. For the "transitional" generation, however, which was born or matured before the oil boom, the state has provided certain services for the population, but it does not have such an omnifarious impact or image. To assure the loyalty of this generation, the state, though not claiming perfection, portrays itself as the only alternative to chaos and implicitly asks whether its citizens would rather live under an Iraqi or Syrian government or, even worse, the Iranian regime.

Achieving a balance between changing internal expectations and external threats is complicated. Although the regime has the ability to institute certain changes to enhance its authority, it frequently is unable to control the total impact of those changes or often to foresee all the implications of its actions. A principal impetus in the creation of the Kuwaiti National Assembly was the threat to Kuwaiti independence in 1961 by Iraq's claim that Kuwaiti ruler Shaykh 'Abdullah al-Salim Al Sabah was simply an Iraqi subordinate like other Iraqi governors. Rather than contesting his personal independence, Shaykh 'Abdullah established a National Assembly that legitimized a separate, sovereign state. The threat to national sovereignty seemingly has forged a closer relationship or intimation of a partnership between the ruling Al Sabah family and other elements of the Kuwaiti population. At the same time, it has produced tensions between a citizenry insistent on full partnership in governing and a ruling family reluctant to relinquish power.

The Nature of Political Participation

Political participation can be defined as "a process whereby individuals engage in activity that impinges directly upon the national power and authority structure of society."[13] Such activity can either challenge the system or support it. In the latter case, "large numbers of individuals come to support an authority structure to which they have meaningful access and which represents their interests" and, as the process of participation deepens, "the political elite will persistently both encourage and meet [increasing social and political] demands for expanding representation."[14]

By their written constitutions, the GCC states describe themselves as democratic, implying a commitment to political participation. The term "democracy" is not without ambiguity in the Western context, let alone in an Arab, Muslim, newly emerging political environment. There is little reason to suppose that the Arab monarchies of the Gulf will be transformed, either voluntarily or violently, into Western-style parliamentary democracies in the foreseeable future. Clearly, rulers and ruling families will continue to exercise paramount power into the long term. The relevant questions concern a foreseeable or expected devolution of power: How much power will be shared, how it will be shared, and with whom it will be shared?

A prevalent assumption, based on Western historical experience, holds that these political systems must be evolutionary. According to this view, changing expectations and increasing demands for fuller participation in all aspects of political life eventually will force the transformation of these polities, either through a voluntary dispersion of power on the part of ruling families or by dissidence and revolution. This assumption, however, may display a normative bias toward conceptions of Western-style democracy as a more just form of government and therefore a desirable consequence of political development.

On the one hand, monarchies generally are regarded as anachronistic in the latter half of the twentieth century. The demise of existing monarchies, found today almost exclusively in the Middle East, and often, if erroneously, described as "absolute monarchies," is held to be inevitable. The weight of history is shown by reference to the demise of other Middle Eastern monarchies over the course of the twentieth century, and modern states are considered incompatible with a monarchical form of government. The Arab Gulf states are assumed to represent a clear-cut dichotomy of rulers and ruled that cannot last, either for the medium term or the long run.

On the other hand, these states are not historic fossils or colonial creations but the product of changing attitudes, outlooks, and expectations. Far from being absolute monarchs in the manner of Louis XIV, the Gulf's rulers govern under the constraints of the *shari'a*, customary and constitutional law, consensus within the ruling family, and consideration of popular expectations. Other than in the overt form of government, distinctions are blurred between governors and governed, between elites and non-elites, and even in terms of class. It is exceedingly difficult to define elites in the Arab Gulf states with their small homogeneous native populations. Historically, most sectors of society existed on a roughly equal footing with ruling families. Today, the majority of the citizenry displays characteristics of an emerging middle class or bourgeoisie.[15]

More accurately, perhaps, the citizenry of the Arab Gulf states can be viewed as an aristocracy, with the ruling families forming an upper stratum that preserves the right to rule within their ranks. The working class is composed principally of expatriates who are not considered members of the society and whose political voice and long-term requirements and demands need not be addressed by the state. Political participation, then, takes place only within the "aristocracy" of the indigenous population.

The extent of participation forms part of a continuing political dialectic between the regime and the citizenry that is most apparent in Kuwait and Bahrain, probably because of their longer exposure to the impact of oil-fueled socioeconomic change and their historical record of political agitation. The direct and personal relationship between ruler and ruled has been lost as the state has grown more complex. Simultaneously, the process of institutionalization has forced the ruler to delegate authority to close family members and state organs, and the state's power over its population has expanded even as participation in decision making has contracted. These changes have created an imbalance in the relationship between ruler and ruled. An ideological schism has appeared between a ruling family basing its claim to leadership on historical rights and an urbanized population seeking to make the government accountable through elected representatives.

The first demands of participation along nontraditional lines preceded the impact of oil. In Kuwait and Bahrain, these demands originated in the 1920s. The 1938 reform movements in Kuwait, Bahrain, and Dubai appear to have been inspired by the currents of constitutionalism and Arab nationalism percolating through the Middle East during that period.[16] The social change engendered by oil wealth, with its opportunities for development, education, travel, changing lifestyles, and personal goals, has refocused, and in some cases intensified, demands for political participation. Only the rush of oil wealth and the emphasis on material improvement in the 1970s muted these demands. Although differences are virtually invisible on the surface, the dialectic between regime and citizenry has become more problematic, and a solution to the still-subdued contest over effective participation in decision making is much more difficult to discern.

Regimes still cling to the mythology of "traditional," "tribal," or social democracy as the basis of their relationship with their people. The claim that the Arab Gulf societies are built on "traditional" democracy is made through reference to the institutions of *majlis*, *shura*, and *ijma'*. Although most prominent people hold a regular *majlis* for social and business purposes, the *majlis*es of rulers, other members of ruling families, government ministers, and local governors also have political implications. Such gatherings constitute a forum in which officials and populace mix, petitions are presented, grievances are made known, opinions are exchanged, and information is gathered by the ruling elite. By this means and other informal discussion with members of basic constituencies and their own families, the rulers are held to have fulfilled the Islamic requirement of consultation.

In many respects, this concept represents a deliberately maintained mythology. The idealized concept of political organization rests on the tribe as the basic unit, with tribal leadership vested in the shaykh, who served not as ruler but as "chairman," a mediator, and conciliator within the tribe and its spokesman to the outside world. In theory, the shaykh was chosen in democratic fashion, but more often he took power by hereditary descent from within an aristocratic clan. The more powerful clans, relying on the size and strength of their own tribe, wealth, possession of a special religious status (such as the role of the Al Sa'ud as propagators of the Wahhabi movement), or alliance with outside actors (such as that of the trucial shaykhs of the Gulf coast with the British), gradually extended their influence and authority over allied tribes. Eventually, paramount shaykhs became *hakim*s (rulers) of defined territories.

The putative egalitarianism between the shaykhly families and their populace, always ambiguous at best, clearly had been suppressed by the early part of the twentieth century. Oil income then transformed the relationship into one of ruler and ruled. The basic viability of this new relationship is likely to endure as long as the political mythology is generally accepted, the ruling elite governs beneficially, and material benefits are forthcoming and distributed in a roughly equal manner. At the same time, however, the mythology may be malleable as conceptions of the political structure and expectations of the government's role change. This is a gradual process, requiring a series of adjustments, rather than an abrupt question of the legitimacy of the regime and political system. In part, the malleability may be due to the maintenance of a certain degree of participation within the system. It can even be argued that, as an aristocracy or elite, the indigenous inhabitants are silent partners in a political system that serves their interests implicitly.

Decision making in all the GCC states, however, is the

preserve of an extremely small elite. The elite is composed of members of ruling families in the first instance and of a small group of "civil servants" or technocrats, drawn largely from prominent merchant families, in the second instance. The size and composition of this elite was determined in the first decade of each country's creation and development of present government infrastructures. Since then, there has been very little penetration of this circle, and most of the same decision makers have held the same or similar positions since those formative years. A look at the cabinets of Saudi Arabia, Bahrain, Qatar, and Oman demonstrates the longevity of the elite. The continued vacancy of four key positions in the Qatari cabinet is due to the lack of suitable candidates within the various branches of the Al Thani designated to hold those portfolios.

There has been relatively greater mobility in the Kuwaiti and UAE cabinets. In the case of Kuwait, this has been due to a combination of a longer history of cabinets and a larger pool of, as well as greater receptivity to, technically qualified candidates. As the same time, cabinet members from the Al Sabah have tended to hold the same positions since independence except where changes have been rendered necessary due to death; Sabah al-Ahmad, for example, is the longest-serving foreign minister in the world. In the UAE, greater mobility has been occasioned by the need to accommodate ruling-family members and other qualified candidates from all seven amirates, as well as by the change in the philosophy that reserved nearly all cabinet positions for ruling families. Nevertheless, the key positions remain in the hands of sons of Shaykh Rashid ibn Sa'id Al Maktum and the Bani Muhammad of the Al Nahyan.

Such narrowness in the decision-making process leads to stagnation in outlook, particularly as it affects the development process, and, potentially, to alienation. Some nationals have suggested that the cabinets by necessity have turned into councils of yes-men because their members are obliged to protect what they have done in office. Periodic new blood, while healthy for the country, represents a threat to the existing system and those presently holding office. Some argue that not only would new members correct mistakes made by the existing cabinets, but they would be more careful to do things right because they, in turn, would be answerable to their successors.

There are several aspects of active participation in these systems. First, rulers are not absolute monarchs, but their families form the primary decision-making bodies of the state, bodies that influence and occasionally contradict rulers. As large entities, these ruling families display a wide variety of opinions, strategies, and goals. Factions within the families may be influenced by certain sectors of the populace and may seek to either curry support from sympathetic sectors or maneuver against rival family factions through manipulation of sectors of the general population.

Second, there is traditional participation through the institutions of *majlis* and *shura*. Third, informal participation occurs as a result of institutional expansion. Nonmembers of ruling families, by dint of their education and personal qualifications, occupy prominent and influential positions in the government, including key cabinet and military posts. Although they may not make the final decisions themselves, they are often in a position to influence those decisions and to shape and present to the rulers the available options.

Fourth, indirect participation occurs in some states through the activities of public and semipublic organizations, including social and sports clubs, student organizations, and professional societies. Fifth, specialized public or quasi-government bodies, such as municipal councils and chambers of commerce, influence decisions and often have elected members and leaders. Finally, all but one of the independent GCC states have had formal national councils on the national level, with elections in the past for those in Kuwait and Bahrain.

The limited nature of these forms of participation, including the troubled history of elected parliaments, demonstrates that the Gulf states are not true democracies, at least in the Western sense of the word. The decline of traditional democratic institutions and the marginal impact of modern participatory institutions have resulted in a dearth of acceptable means of legitimate dissent. The recent decades of development orientation have seen small, tightly knit groups of individuals making fundamental decisions, particularly in the economic and industrial spheres, that will have continuing impact on the countries for generations to come. Although government actions and decisions in general appear to enjoy the approval of the great majority of the populations, some dissent does exists over specific decisions and economic strategies. Channels for voicing criticism, let alone receiving genuine government consideration of such criticism, are rudimentary at best, however.

Although circumscribed and severely restricted, dissent in the GCC states can be voiced in various ways and is still tolerated by regimes. It is, however, quite easy to overstep the boundaries. Means of dissent include the following:

• *Informal Majlis.* More than just a social gathering, the informal *majlis* (or *diwan* or *diwaniya*) is an institution in which personal relationships are maintained and strengthened, business is conducted, and politics is discussed. Even in the official *majlis*es of government officials, subtle criticism can be expressed and public opinion on an issue gauged.[17]

• *Press and Public Lectures.* Until the assembly suspension in July 1986, Kuwait's five daily Arabic newspapers were lively sources of reporting and political opinion on Kuwait and the other Gulf states. Sharjah's *al-Khalij* displays a strongly iconoclastic, pan-Arabist orientation and regularly publishes articles by Gulf political figures, including Kuwaiti "leftists."[18] Newspapers and other UAE forums sponsor talks by controversial Kuwaiti, Bahraini, and UAE speakers, and student groups at Kuwait University offer lectures in which political problems are actively discussed.

The other GCC states are far more restrictive in their implicit censorship of political discussion. Ghazi al-Gosaibi's publication of a critical poem in a Saudi newspaper crossed over the acceptable boundary and resulted in his demotion from minister of health to ambassador to Bahrain.

• *Clubs, Societies, and Religious Institutions.* In earlier decades, students returning from abroad established cultural clubs, which served to transmit political ideas and opinions. Cultural and literary clubs with political overtones first appeared in Bahrain and Kuwait in the 1920s and 1930s. In both countries, certain clubs organized political movements in the 1950s and 1960s to protest government policies, and later candidates for election lobbied clubs for votes. Clubs and professional societies also serve as agents of socialization among generations, social strata, and religious or ethnic groups. Particularly for minorities, the congregation of the community in religious institutions (such as the Shi'i *ma'tam* [funeral house]) provides for the discussion of grievances and the formulation of strategies to combat them. As the strongholds of the established merchant community, whose power may have been eclipsed by ruling families in recent decades but who are not without considerable influence, chambers of commerce play quasi-political roles as lobbyists.

• *National Councils.* Formal assemblies have functioned in all of the GCC states except Saudi Arabia, either as elected quasi-parliaments or as advisory councils. But, generally representation by popular vote has succeeded only in voluntary associations, such as clubs and professional societies, which are not subject to government intervention. The government has always been represented in national councils by appointed functionaries with the same rights and privileges as elected members. The regimes thereby have been able to control these institutions, but at the cost of considerable friction. To end the friction, the regimes sooner or later have dissolved the bodies they have established.[19]

• *Strikes and Demonstrations.* To a certain extent, reform activities in the twentieth century were tied to economic grievances, particularly among pearl divers at first and then later in the oil sector. Since the onset of the oil boom, though, strikes have become rare because of the non-participation of nationals in strikes and the increasing effectiveness of security forces.

• *Subversive Organizations and Activities.* For those frustrated by the ineffectiveness of acceptable channels of dissent, there is always the alternative: participation in illegal organizations and activities. The great majority of Gulf citizens have not chosen this path and it is not likely that they will do so in the foreseeable future. Nevertheless, even a tiny radicalized minority can carry out acts with considerable psychological impact on regimes and on public opinion, as demonstrated by the discovery of a number of antigovernment plots in Bahrain since 1981, the 1985 bombings in Riyadh, and the involvement of several indigenous Shi'a in the 1987 bombings in Kuwait.

Official attitudes toward dissent may involve several strategies. First, states may display some limited toleration of subtle criticism, especially if it comes from respected members of the community such as prominent merchants or, especially, the *'ulama'* (religious leaders). Second, regimes may attempt to channel criticism into regime-supporting or at least nonthreatening modes, as in permitting debate over the role and function of expatriates in the society.

Third, states may seek to co-opt critics, a preferable and usually successful alternative to repression. Former rebels sit in the Omani cabinet, a vocal critic of Bahraini government policy in the 1960s is now a minister, and the Kuwaiti regime disarmed at least one parliamentary critic by appointing him to a cabinet position. Fourth, states may rely on repression or intimidation, although this is clearly seen as a last resort and is not widely used. Restrictive actions taken against dissenters, such as their removal from government jobs, revocation of their passports, or house arrest, are often temporary reactions and are later replaced by co-optation.

It is a fair question to ask whether the GCC states can accept, or tolerate, constructive dissent, let alone democracy. The nostalgic and mythologized argument that they possess a "tribal" or "social" democracy becomes increasingly specious as traditional ways disappear. Nevertheless, the opposite argument—that these monarchical regimes are anachronistic, repressive, and autocratic—is belied by their commitment to socioeconomic development and by their citizenry's apparent belief in their legitimacy. They are, however, authoritarian, and the acceptance of such tradition-based authoritarianism in a post-traditional era is likely to diminish as the societies grow and change.

The Roles National Councils Play in the GCC

Are formal national councils, whether parliaments or consultative councils, appropriate for these states? Or are these institutions basically Western imports with no legitimate basis in Gulf societies? This latter does not seem to be the case. Instead, the national councils of the Gulf are attempts to transform traditional informal institutions (even if they are largely mythological) into modern formal institutions. These institutions are intended to legitimize the regime and at least provide the appearance of participation by all sectors of the citizenry in the state-building process during a period of rapid, difficult, and potentially destabilizing change.

The appearance in 1938 of reform movements, complete with attempts to create national councils, at three different places in the Gulf—Kuwait, Bahrain, and Dubai—provides evidence of an indigenous desire for such organs of formal political participation. That all three movements failed is explained by the impetuousness and inexperience of the reformers as much as by the repression of the rulers, not to mention their premature manifestation in societies that had been barely touched by social and political change.

National councils have functioned in all of the GCC states except Saudi Arabia (see table 2). Tentative moves toward a consultative council have been made in Saudi Arabia on various occasions in the last quarter-century, but the government has never carried through on its promises of imminent formation. Only two national councils have approached the status of elected parliaments: Kuwait's National Assembly, twice suspended, most recently in July 1986, and Bahrain's National Assembly, which functioned only briefly in the mid-1970s before it too was suspended. The bodies in Qatar, the UAE, and Oman are largely advisory, with appointed members and little statutory power. Notwithstanding their severe limitations as democratic institutions, these national councils do provide useful and important functions.

The need and demand for formal national councils were limited in the past and may still remain low on the list of state priorities, yet the seeds of future expectations for democratic institutions are being sown now. The record of the two national assemblies has been notably unsuccessful to date, and the only functioning national councils in the GCC at present are consultative or advisory councils. These may exercise a modicum of legislative review and some other functions, but essentially they exist to legitimate the regime and provide a safety valve for the expression of discontent.

The key to the acceptance of these councils as legitimate democratic participatory bodies in the future lies in their record of effectiveness and growth over the coming years. Without national councils, even in restricted form, the future is more likely to center on confrontation over the issue of political participation rather than on cooperation.[20] Conversely, the reduction of ostensibly democratic institutions throughout the Middle East to state-manipulated, ineffective, and, in the end, irrelevant organs will rob regimes

TABLE 2
The National Councils in the Gulf Cooperation Council

	Kuwait National Assembly	Bahrain National Assembly	Qatar Advisory Council	UAE Federal National Council	Oman State Consultative Council
Legal Basis in Constitution?	yes	yes	yes	yes	no
Present Status	suspended	suspended	functioning	functioning	functioning
Term of Office	4 years	4 years	indefinite	2 years	2 years
Selected Members	50	30	30	40	55
Means of Selection	elected	elected	appointed	appointed	appointed
Includes Cabinet?	yes	yes	no	no	no
Council Leaders	elected by members	elected by members	appointed by state	appointed by state	appointed by state
Parties Permitted?	no	no	no	no	no
Legislative Review?	yes	yes	yes	yes	yes
Approves Budget?	yes	yes	yes	yes	no
Has Power to Override Veto?	yes	yes	no	no	no

24

of a valuable intermediary between dissatisfaction and revolution.

Admittedly, there is a world of difference between the two suspended parliaments (even with their restrictions) and the other advisory councils. Nevertheless, given their creation in similar circumstances, they all encompass many of the same functions, albeit to different degrees, and thus are worthy of comparison and generalization. At least six formal or informal functions encompassed by the GCC's national councils can be discerned, as introduced below.

1. *Legitimation of the Regime.* A national council, generally styled as a parliament or similar "democratic" institution, has become *de rigueur* for nearly all regimes. At the very least, it preserves the facade of constitutional legitimacy and implies a "social contract" between the government and its citizenry.

2. *Formalized Majlis.* Consciously or not, some national councils appear to be efforts to reconstruct the traditional informal *majlis* in a formal, constitutional manner.

3. *Legislative Role.* Formal participation in the legislative process, let alone the right to debate government policy, initiate or defeat legislation, and override executive vetoes, has existed only in the two elected parliaments. Elsewhere, limited functions of legislative review have been introduced at the prerogative of the rulers, sometimes with the privilege of questioning ministers.

4. *Government Accountability.* The written constitutions of the Gulf specify that sovereignty rests with the people. Theoretically then, governments are accountable to the people. Given the hereditary nature of rulers, their selection from chosen families, and their accepted right to appoint and dismiss cabinets, the only constitutional means of accountability rests within national councils. In a general sense, the legislative powers of these bodies constitute a check on government policies and activities. More specifically, accountability rests with the ability of the na-

tional councils to question responsible members of government about their personal actions or the activities of their ministry.

5. *Incipient Populism.* In an age when government has become impersonal and the average citizen deals not with the ruler directly but with an entrenched bureaucracy, national councils can provide an outlet for the expression of opinions and grievances. They can act as a safety valve. As a result, members of national councils throughout the Gulf frequently have adopted a populist stance, speaking out on behalf of the "little guy," particularly when perceptions are strong that the poorer citizens are being hurt by the economic recession and resultant government policies. It appears to be in the interest of the governments to encourage this incipient populism, insofar as it counteracts the growing possibility of alienation and provides at least a facade of popular participation and representation.

6. *Legitimation of Political Participation by Minority or Non-Elite Groups.* Sectarian and ethnic minorities have been represented (and perhaps over represented) in the various bodies of the Gulf, either through election by fellow members of their communities or by the conscious efforts of governments to provide these groups with representation. The representatives then gain high public profile by their membership and activities in the bodies.

Each of the national councils will be analyzed in terms of these functions and some general conclusions will be made in the concluding chapter.

2

Kuwait

The genesis of national councils in Kuwait in the 1920s and 1930s more resembled the struggle between the English barons and King John that lead to the Magna Carta of 1215 than it did a truly democratic movement. The early efforts of prominent Kuwaiti notables and merchants to create consultative councils were aimed principally at restoring the balance of oligarchy traditionally enjoyed with the ruling Al Sabah family. Not until independence and the establishment of the National Assembly (*Majlis al-Umma*) did the roots of transformation to democratic representation begin to replace the fading oligarchic and growing authoritarian nature of Kuwaiti politics. Kuwait's National Assembly was the first and the longest-serving national council in the GCC states. Apart from the short-lived Bahraini National Assembly, it has been the only reasonably authentic legislature to date. But the path to a modern parliament has not been smooth, and the National Assembly was suspended in July 1986 for the second time in its history.

Background

Kuwait's apparent willingness to experiment more fully than its neighbors with democratic institutions is due to several factors. Most important of these are Kuwait's unique historical background and the relative longevity of its oil-fueled socioeconomic development. Modern Kuwait derives from the eighteenth-century migration of several families of the 'Utub tribe from central Arabia to what is now Kuwait City.[1] The new 'Utaybi settlement waxed prosperous on its growing status as an entrepôt, utilizing its natural harbor (and freedom from the political disruptions that plagued competing ports), the seafaring skills of its inhabitants, and fulfillment of the commercial needs of a tribal, bedouin hinterland.

Control of the emerging mercantile state was in the hands of an oligarchy of notable families. These Sunni Arab families of respected central Arabian tribal origin continue to form the elite of Kuwait, together with other Sunni and Shi'i merchant families who migrated to Kuwait more recently. Sabah al-Jabir was chosen from their ranks as the community's political leader and his family, the Al Sabah, have provided the rulers of Kuwait ever since.

By the turn of the twentieth century, however, the partnership between the Al Sabah and the other founding fathers was threatened by the autocratic attitude of Shaykh Mubarak Al Sabah (r. 1896–1915) and his sons Jabir (r. 1915–1917) and Salim (r. 1917–1921), who had abandoned the informal practice of consultation with non-Al Sabah notables. In addition, the growing exposure of some Kuwaitis to the outside world, particularly among the well-traveled and educated merchant community, gave rise to a desire for a new, formal consultative council.

The 1921 Council

Popular feeling was running high in 1921 against Shaykh Salim. His customs dispute with Ibn Sa'ud, ruler of the Najd and later king of Saudi Arabia, and the depredations of the Ikhwan (the religious warriors originally promoted by Ibn Sa'ud) had caused a severe loss of trade, a situation further inflamed by Shaykh Salim's lackluster administration, lack of tact, and neglect of the tradition of consultation. A group of Kuwaiti notables seized the occasion of his death in 1921 to push the Al Sabah family to agree to the establishment of a consultative council with the ruler at its head, at least partially with the hope of influencing the succession. Twelve representatives of the merchant community were appointed to the new council and a leading merchant, Hamad al-Saqr, served as chairman. A few meetings apparently were held with the new ruler, Shaykh Ahmad (r. 1921–1950), but these were desultory and the council was reduced to internal quarreling. By 1928, membership had fallen to six (including two Al Sabah), and, moribund, the council eventually faded away.[2]

Despite the failure of this first attempt at formal participation, Kuwait was increasingly affected by the ideas of nationalism and constitutionalism then buffeting the Arab world, and demands for political reform were soon to resurface. A Municipal Council was created in 1930 and its dozen members were elected in subsequent years. Their relationship with the ruler was often stormy, and, in 1934, the ruler had the elected chairman, Sulayman al-'Adsani, replaced. Two years later, an election was held for the Education Council. When the ruler dissolved the latter council and installed an appointed one, the Municipal Council resigned en masse.[3]

The 1938 Council

These events proved to be a prelude to the renewed attempt to institute an elected consultative council in 1938.[4] The ruler's tightfistedness, both in expenditures on state services and in the allowances provided Al Sabah family members, his lack of attention to administration and justice, his retention of state income and fears that he would not share potential oil revenues (the first strike occurred in February 1938), the rigging of municipality elections, the loss of trade caused by the continuing Saudi blockade, the absence of development efforts, and a decade of Iraqi agitation against Al Sabah rule all contributed to the underlying discontent. Shaykh Ahmad's autocratic penchant, characterized by his treatment of the mid-1930s councils, fueled the growing dissatisfaction and forced some Kuwaitis in exile in Iraq to form parties such as *al-Shabiba* and the National Bloc. Nebulous groups began to argue variously for the replacement of the ruler by the heir apparent, protection from the ruler by the assumption of a British protectorate for the shaykhdom, and political union with Iraq. 'Abd al-Hamid al-Sani' was arrested in September 1937, thus becoming Kuwait's first political prisoner.

The tension escalated into a crisis upon the public flogging of Muhammad al-Barrak in mid-March 1938 for propaganda against the ruler and for "intriguing." Al-Barrak's associates, members of leading merchant families who had long discussed the need for a representative council, became fearful of reprisals; some sought British protection and others fled to Iraq. The National Bloc published a seven-point reform program in an Iraqi newspaper. Meanwhile, Shaykh Ahmad stubbornly denied the existence of public dissatisfaction and brushed aside a British protest over the flogging, as well as suggestions for reforms, appointment of an adviser, and reinstitution of an elected council.

Finally, in the face of petitions from leading notables and continued British pressure, Shaykh Ahmad agreed to the formation of a council. A committee formed a list of eligible voters from 150 Kuwaiti families, who elected a 14-person council (*Majlis al-Umma al-Tashri'i*) on June 29 with heir apparent Shaykh 'Abdullah al-Salim as its chairman.[5] A first order of business was the drafting of an interim constitution, modeled on the 1923 Egyptian constitution. After insistence by family members, Shaykh Ahmad signed the document on July 6, 1938.[6]

In its early days, the council turned its attention to economic reforms – revising customs regulations to encourage trade – and administrative changes – including the creation of finance and police departments, the opening of three schools and arranging for importing additional teachers, the replacement of corrupt government employees and judges, the formation of a new, elected municipal council, and the abolition of pearling taxes and forced labor. Confrontation with the ruler came early when the council demanded that Shaykh Ahmad fire his Persian *wazir* or factotum (who apparently had been attempting to raise a Shi'a-Persian countermovement to the all-Sunni council) and his Syrian secretary, 'Izzat Ja'far. The ruler adamantly refused, and the prospect of armed clashes loomed before the *wazir* and secretary were sent away on indefinite leave. The council was then able to take control of the payment of Al Sabah allowances out of customs revenues and the ruler agreed to turn over the oil company payment when he received it in December.

Despite the promising start, the council lasted barely six months. It had arrogated too much power for itself, instituted too many reforms too quickly, acted ambiguously over the issue of unity with Iraq, and failed to cultivate popular support for its contest with the ruler. It faced resistance from naturally conservative segments of the population, as well as the bedouin, the Shi'a, those secretly encouraged by the ruler, merchants who had lost monopolies through council reforms, outlying villagers (the sale of whose produce was threatened by council regulations), and even by a council member involved in business dealings with the ruler's entourage.

Shaykh Ahmad also resisted the council's attempts to write a sweeping permanent constitution that would severely constrain the ruler's powers. Matters reached a head on December 21, 1938 when Shaykh Ahmad announced his intention to dissolve the council and its members retreated to the fort in Kuwait. After tense negotiations, the council surrendered and acquiesced in its dissolution in return for the ruler's agreement to hold new elections, albeit with a proviso by which he could veto its decisions.

A few days later, an electorate of 400 chose a new 20-member council. Twelve members of the old council were reelected, as well as a conservative (who had resigned from the earlier council), four supporters of the ruler, two apparent supporters of the council, and one neutral.[7] Before convening the council, Shaykh Ahmad abrogated the old constitution and announced a new one giving him veto rights, thus effectively transforming the council from an executive body to an advisory one. Not surprisingly, the council refused to accept the change. It had yet to meet when the ruler dissolved it on March 7, 1939, after he had regained control of the arsenal.

Three days later, a water carrier named Muhammad al-Munayyis attracted a crowd when he began speaking against the ruler and handing out leaflets calling for the overthrow of the Al Sabah. As he was being led to jail, two members of the old council, Yusuf al-Marzuq and Muhammad al-Qitami, scuffled with his guards in an attempt to release al-Munayyis. Al-Marzuq apparently aimed a revolver at the bedouin guards who returned fire, wounding Marzuq and a nearby shopkeeper and killing al-Qitami. The decision was made to restore order by trying, convicting, and executing Munayyis (presumably of treason). The following day, five members of the old council were arrested along with a number of other people, while at least a dozen individuals (including several council members) fled to exile in Iraq.[8] On March 12, Shaykh Ahmad initiated the final move in the drama by appointing a 13-member advisory council under the leadership of Shaykh 'Abdullah al-Salim; nine members were to be nominated by the ruler and the other four were from the Al Sabah family. The council convened on the following day.[9] Shaykh Ahmad clearly had emerged triumphant over the democratic movement, while his newly appointed and ineffective council soon faded away.

Further attempts at political reform were equally ineffective. The crushing of the leaders of the 1938 movement, the deflection of Iraq's attention by World War II and internal divisions, and the merchant community's preoccupation with economic opportunities all contributed to the relative lessening of demands for representation. Oil production surged forward in the 1950s but virtually the entire government remained in the hands of four senior Al Sabah.

Elections were held in 1952 and 1954 for 12-member advisory committees for the municipality, health, education, and *awqaf* (religious endowments), but only the head of the Education Department cooperated with his council and the others failed to function effectively. In 1954, the disappointing showing of these councils in curtailing the abuses of the members of the ruling families in charge of these departments, as well as the slowdown in development after the rapid pace of the previous year, prompted the merchants to present the ruler with a petition for the reform of the administration, including a Central Council to be formed of selected representatives from the elected councils.[10] In response, the amir formed a Higher Executive Committee (HEC—*al-Hay'a al-Tanfidhiya al-'Ulya*) to reorganize the administration, but it was not well regarded and had to contend with the amir's influential uncle, 'Abdullah al-Mubarak.[11] As a consequence, pamphlets attacking the committee and calling for a national council were distributed in the name of the Kuwait Democratic League and other organizations.[12]

In May 1955, Dr. Ahmad Muhammad al-Khatib's weekly newspaper, *Sada al-Iman*, collected signatures to a petition for an elected assembly.[13] A meeting to elect members of a People's Executive Committee was called but was banned by the government. Eventually, a five-member delegation headed by al-Khatib was received by the ruler, who accepted their petition.[14] These events prompted a secret council of the six most senior members of the ruling family on November 2 to discuss the growing popular discontent over the government's disorganization and public criticism of the behavior of some Al Sabah and to attempt to unite the family and determine what concessions were to be made.[15] The ruler, 'Abdullah al-Salim, responded to the failure of the HEC by creating a Family Council in November 1955, later known as the Supreme Council (*al-Majlis al-A'la*). Formal meetings were held on a weekly basis and the council was able to make considered decisions on the basis of prepared agenda papers, as well as deal with individual complaints against government departments. Initially composed of the senior family members who were also heads of departments, the council was intended to eventually include other government officials, and it served as a surrogate for a cabinet until independence in 1961.[16]

Discontent continued to simmer through the 1950s over the indecision and apparent misdirection of the Kuwaiti government, and a close watch was kept on political events in nearby Bahrain. The discontent was expressed in the activities of the National Cultural, Graduates, and Teachers Clubs, in such weekly newspapers as *Sada al-Iman* and *Akhbar al-Usbu'* and in public meetings. The government moved quickly to suppress such activities by censoring the newspapers and so forcing them to cease publication and by issuing warnings of imprisonment to the leaders of the clubs.[17]

Even though government reforms were gradually instituted, another attempt to revive a national council in 1957 was equally unsuccessful. Nevertheless, organized political opposition continued to proliferate. Imported Egyptian teachers laid the groundwork for the establishment of a local Muslim Brotherhood organization in 1951, the progenitor of the current Social Reform Society. Young Kuwaiti liberals gravitated to the Teachers Club, founded in 1951, and the more pan-Arab-oriented Cultural Club, organized in 1952, and Graduates' Club, established in 1955. Ba'this, influenced by Syrian and Palestinian expatriates, formed the Union Club during the same period, and the Kuwait Democratic Youth, a Communist organization particularly strong among the Iraqi and Iranian communities, dates from the early 1950s. Kuwaiti nationalists founded the Kuwaiti Students Union in 1957, while Kuwaiti opposition ranks were strengthened with the arrival of exiles from Bahrain following the suppression of the nationalist movement there in 1956.[18]

External events sparked political demonstrations. The British intervention in Suez on October 29, 1956 prompted a general strike and the resignation of a number of Kuwaiti officials, led by Colonel Jasim al-Qattami, the director of the police force, and 10 of his men. In a possibly related event, saboteurs set off 10 explosions around the Ahmadi oil camp and the nearby oil port.[19] A meeting in February 1959 to celebrate the anniversary of Egypt and Syria's union in the United Arab Republic attracted thousands and resulted in the withdrawal of the passports of Jasim al-Qattami and other speakers and the deportation of hundreds.[20] It was not until after independence that this period of political suppression ended and a number of opposition figures were co-opted with important government positions.

Independence and the Establishment of the National Assembly

The impact of Amir 'Abdullah al-Salim on the formation of modern Kuwait is manifold. During his rule came the first dramatic stages of extensive socioeconomic change and the physical transformation of Kuwait. The bold decision to institute a parliament shortly after independence was another consequence of his reign. In part, the decision reflected concern over the prevailing currents of pan-Arab nationalism and the influence of the many expatriate Arabs on Kuwaiti opinion. It also seems to have been a defensive reaction to the recrudescence of Iraqi claims to the amirate on the eve of Kuwaiti independence. At the same time, the legacy of political activism from the 1930s had left its mark on the nation's consciousness, including on the amir who, after all, had been the chosen president of the 1938 council.[21]

The Constituent Assembly (1962) and the Constitution

The Anglo-Kuwaiti note of June 19, 1961 terminated Kuwait's status as a British-protected state, a situation that had existed since 1899, and gave the amirate full independence. Soon after, a committee of senior Al Sabah members and representatives of the merchant community was formed to make preparations for an elected constituent assembly. The new assembly's 20 seats were contested by 74 candidates in the election of December 30, 1961; the inclusion of the cabinet ministers as ex-officio members raised total membership to 31. Although the assembly acted as a provisional legislature with some restricted functions, its principal role was to draft the country's permanent constitution. The Constituent Assembly first met on January 20, 1962 and was dissolved after it submitted the constitution to the amir, who signed it on November 11, 1962.[22]

Although the constitution affirmed Kuwait's political system as a hereditary monarchy under the Al Sabah (and formally restricted succession to the descendants of Amir Mubarak the Great, Art. 4), it also instituted significant restrictions on the ruler's power. The amir is given the authority to nominate his successor subject to the approval of the National Assembly (Art. 4); the citizens' right to social and economic welfare and opportunity is guaranteed (Arts. 7–24); the deportation of Kuwaitis is prohibited (Art. 28) and personal liberties are guaranteed (Art. 30); the freedom of the press, residences, and communications is stipulated (Arts. 37–39), as well as the right of private and public assembly (Art. 44) and for citizens to petition the authorities in writing (Art. 45). The system of government is based on the separation of powers, with executive power vested in the amir and cabinet (replacing the Supreme Council of senior Al Sabah family members who hitherto had headed all principal agencies), legislative power shared by the amir and a National Assembly, and judicial power held independently by the courts (Arts. 50–53, 162–163).

Perhaps the most radical innovations of the constitution concerned the role of the elected National Assembly. The assembly consists of 50 members elected by secret ballot (Art. 80), as well as all nonelected cabinet ministers as ex officio members (Art. 81). Members must be Kuwaiti by origin, qualified as an elector, 30 years old, and literate in

Arabic (Art. 82). The assembly term is set at four calendar years, with elections for the new assembly taking place within 60 days (Art. 83). The amir may dissolve the assembly once but must call for new elections within two months (Art. 107). Assembly members may put questions to the prime minister and the other ministers and raise debate on matters within their competence (Arts. 99–100), and individual ministers are subject to votes of no-confidence (Art. 101), although only the amir has the right to demand the resignation of the prime minister or the cabinet as a whole (Art. 102).

Clearly, the assembly was envisaged as the representative of the citizenry in a political contract between the ruler and the people. Before assuming office, the amir is directed to swear an oath to respect the constitution and defend the state before a special session of the assembly (Art. 60). Ministers are to be appointed from assembly members and others and the cabinet is not to exceed one-third the members of the assembly (Art. 56), a safeguard against packing votes in the assembly. Laws may be promulgated only after being passed by the National Assembly and sanctioned by the amir (Art. 79), and the assembly can override the amir's veto by a two-thirds majority (Art. 66). The assembly must approve the state's annual budget (Art. 140), and a two-thirds majority and the approval of the amir is required for revision of the constitution (Art. 174).

The First 14 Years (1963–1976)

The first elections to the National Assembly were held on January 23, 1963, with 205 candidates vying for the votes of 17,000 male citizens for one of the 50 seats.[23] Subsequent elections were held in 1967, 1971, and 1975 before the assembly was suspended in 1976, with the lists of candidates averaging over 200. The number of eligible voters increased to nearly 27,000 in 1967, more than 40,000 in 1971, and nearly 53,000 in 1975, although less than 60 percent actually voted in those elections.[24] The effective functioning of the

National Assembly during these first 14 years was responsible for firmly entrenching a number of fundamental innovations in the Kuwaiti political system.

Even as the cabinet replaced the exclusively Al Sabah
Supreme Council as the state's executive body, cabinet ministers found that they were no longer answerable solely to
the amir. Henceforth their actions and policies were open to
public scrutiny within the assembly. The old oligarchy of
shaykhly families and the merchant elite, which had mo-
nopolized power in Kuwait in the past, found itself sharing
power with the sedentarized bedouin (whose settlement in
Kuwait and citizenship were encouraged by the government
because of their strong loyalty to the Al Sabah) and with
the emerging middle class of businessmen, government officials, professionals, and intellectuals. Nearly a quarter of
the first assembly's members were liberal nationalists, led
by Dr. Ahmad al-Khatib.[25]

Far from being a rubber stamp, the first National Assembly emerged as a forum for criticism of government
policy and the expression of national identity. The Al Sabah
ministers of defense and interior came in for public interrogation of their ministerial policies. The assembly opposed
the validity of the December 1964 cabinet on the grounds
that some of its members were engaged in business in violation of the constitution (Art. 131), and the government was
forced to form a new cabinet in January 1965. The assembly also forced modifications in royalty agreements with
the concessionary oil companies. The increasing success of
the assembly's conservative bloc in late 1965 in passing
legislation provoked the resignation of eight members,
whose seats were filled by progovernment members in February 1966 by-elections. In foreign policy, the nationalists
called for abrogation of the 1961 agreement with Britain for
defense assistance and for negotiations toward Arab unity.[26]

The elections to the second assembly (1967–1971) severely eroded the position of the nationalists. Most of the
26 new members were regarded as conservative and progovernment. Despite having put up 37 candidates, only four

members of the nationalist bloc were reelected; Ahmad al-Khatib was among the defeated. Thirty-eight candidates (including six successful ones) were joined by student and professional organizations in accusing the government of rigging the elections, and seven newly elected members refused their seats in protest.[27] The Arab defeat in the June 1967 war, and by implication the failure of Nasirism and pan-Arabism, was cited as the major reason for the decline of the nationalists, as well as the beginning of influence for the Islamics (*al-Islamiyun*; Islamic ideologues). Although al-Khatib and a few supporters were reelected in the 1980s, they were not able to command the 10 or so votes in the assembly that they had in the 1960s.[28]

The nationalists were able to increase their strength in the 1971 elections, and they played a leading role in pushing for a ceiling on oil production (for conservation reasons) and a more aggressive participation agreement, which gave the Kuwaiti government 60 percent ownership of the oil companies' Kuwaiti operations. In the 1975 elections, nearly half the winners were new to the assembly and the resultant body was younger, better educated, and less conservative than its predecessors.[29]

The First Suspension (1976)

On August 29, 1976, Prime Minister Jabir al-Ahmad Al Sabah submitted his resignation to the amir, who dissolved the National Assembly and placed restrictions on the press on the same day. In addition, he suspended the articles of the constitution requiring a member of the cabinet to be drawn from the elected National Assembly (Art. 57), providing for either new elections within two months or reinstitution of the old assembly (Art. 107), requiring National Assembly approval of any constitutional revisions (Art. 174), and forbidding the suspension of the constitution except under martial law and forbidding the suspension of National Assembly meetings during martial law (Art. 181). In an attempt to justify the suspension, the Lebanese experience was cited as an example of the dangers of political dissension and an unregulated press, and the vocal opposition was singled out as a disruptive factor. As heir apparent, Shaykh Jabir was reappointed prime minister and proceeded to form a new cabinet.

The assembly's opposition groups often had provided an effective counterweight to the government on substantial issues, such as the lack of sufficient public housing, the imposition of ceilings on oil production, and the rejection of government measures for nationalization of the oil industry as not being complete or rapid enough. At the same time, however, the opposition focused undue attention on sensitive and even trivial matters. In his letter of resignation, the prime minister cited the problems caused by the assembly's neglect of legislative matters and the frequency of personal attacks on cabinet ministers. A fear of growing ideological and class conflict was another contributing factor to the dissolution of the assembly. Assembly sessions grew tense during the summer of 1976, with assembly members pointedly accusing ministers of using their posts for personal gain and attacking the continued political and economic domination of Kuwait by the ruling family and a small circle of prominent merchant families.

As in Lebanon, part of the problem arising from Kuwait's relatively free press was the frequent attacks on neighboring countries, which embarrassed the government in its relations with Saudi Arabia, Iraq, Egypt, and Syria. This included press criticism of the government's support for Syria in its then-pro-Maronite role in Lebanon.[30]

The suspension was not only a political matter between the Al Sabah and their opponents within the National Assembly but, more important, a constitutional issue. The arbitrary and unconstitutional suspension of certain articles of the constitution seemed to reduce the institution of parliament in Kuwait to that of a consultative council, carrying no more legitimacy and protection from an amir's fiat than the councils of 1921 and 1938. Amir Sabah promised to restore the National Assembly within four years, but this commitment fell open to debate within the ruling family following the amir's death on December 31, 1977. The al-Salim branch tended to argue against restoration, but the new amir, Shaykh Jabir al-Ahmad, appeared to favor political participation. The formation of a committee in February 1980 to revise the constitution and prepare for elections to the Fifth Assembly, just within the four-year deadline, brought the constitutional crisis to an end. Six years later, the crisis returned with the second suspension of the National Assembly.

Restoration of the National Assembly (1981–1986)

The Fifth National Assembly (1981–1985)

True to the word of his cousin, and despite considerable uncertainty, Amir Jabir set in motion the machinery for the restoration of the National Assembly within the four-year period. That he was not personally opposed to the assembly (unlike other Al Sabah), the popularity of such a move, and the desirability of demonstrating the legitimacy and openness of the regime in the face of the Iranian revolution, which had raised tensions considerably in the amirate, undoubtedly contributed to his decision.

A number of changes in the electoral law accompanied the restoration. The most important of these increased the number of electoral districts from 10, each electing 5 members, to 25, each electing only 2. There were also allegations that the government had gerrymandered the boundaries and sizes (the numbers of eligible voters varied between 3,000 and 13,000) of these districts in order to increase conservative bedouin representation and decrease troublesome nationalist and perhaps Shi'a representation. The regime had perceived the vocal nationalist opposition group in the National Assemblies of the 1960s and 1970s a particularly potent and worrisome threat. Government strategy in restoring the assembly seemed directed at preventing the nationalists from regaining a platform for antigovernment rhetoric, even to the point of permitting more freedom for the Islamics as a counterweight.[31]

Out of the 90,000 Kuwaitis eligible on February 23, 1981, only 42,000 actually voted, the lowest proportional turnout in Kuwaiti history. Although the victory of 13 young technocrats and 4 Islamics may have been expected, the return of 24–27 bedouin loyalists was not an accurate reflection of Kuwait's social structure. The dismal showing of the nationalists (Ahmad al-Khatib was among the defeated and only three won) seemed to substantiate the gerrymandering charges. The Shi'a did even worse: despite putting up a third of the total candidates and having held 10 seats in the previous assembly, only two Shi'a won election.[32]

The Sixth Assembly (1985-1986)

The elections of February 1985 saw 238 candidates contesting the 50 seats. The election of 31 newcomers to the assembly was a good indication that this assembly would be more energetic, sophisticated, and critical than the preceding one. As usual, the government retained control of the voting with the election of bedouin to more than half the seats, where they joined generally progovernment independents and the cabinet. Unofficial primaries were held in some outlying districts to ensure the eventual election of suitable tribal candidates.[33] Nevertheless, the election outcome presaged difficult times ahead. The results seemed to mirror popular concern over the worsening economic situation and government inability to deal with the Suq al-Manakh (the unofficial stock market) crisis.

The incumbent speaker, Muhammad Yusuf al-'Adsani, a former planning minister with strong government support, was one of several prominent members of the previous assembly defeated. His district was won by an Arab nationalist and an Islamic. Although the reappearance of the small bloc of Arab nationalists posed little threat to the government's voting majority, their relative organization as a bloc and their vociferous criticism of government policies made them a controversial element. The election's impact on the Islamics was mixed: several incumbent Islamics were defeated, but the election of others meant their numbers held steady. Shi'i representation increased from two to three. Ahmad al-Sa'dun, an independent but often strong critic of government policy and the deputy speaker in the Fifth Assembly, was selected to succeed al-'Adsani as speaker in the sixth.[34]

Composition of Membership and Alliances

Although there have never been any formal political parties in Kuwait, a majority of the National Assembly has banded together in unofficial blocs in which some coordination of strategy is evident.[35] As table 3 shows, assembly members can be grouped into at least 11 political or ideological classifications. In most cases, underlying social and religious distinctions cut across these lines. For example, there were three Shi'i members of the assembly. Only one could be considered an Islamic activist, however, and his collaboration with Sunni Islamics was minimal. The other two are relatively secularized and fall best into the category of independents.

As many as 27 members could be considered bedouin or tribalists, and these were initially included in the "National Center Group," established in late 1985 to promote the interests of Kuwait's "remote areas," a euphemism for bedouin communities.[36] The ability of the National Center Group to act as a coordinated lobby was limited, however. Although most of the tribalist members could be considered progovernment, their ranks also included Islamics, independents, semi-independents, and Kuwaiti nationalists. The tribal bloc is further fissured by differences in social status and conflicting patterns of alliances between tribes and with the Al Sabah. Increasingly, tribalist candidates are younger and better educated. In the short run, this allows tribes to

TABLE 3
Kuwait: Groupings in Sixth National Assembly

Members/ Sympathizers	Grouping
15	Cabinet ministers not elected
2	Cabinet ministers appointed from elected membership
19	Pro-Government
3	Semi-Independent (support government on major issues)
12	Independent (not aligned to any grouping)
3	Democratic Bloc (al-Tajamma' al-Dimuqrati; also known as al-Tali'a Group; leftist with origins in the Arab Nationalists' Movement)
2	Arab Nationalists ("liberals," emphasis on Kuwait's role within the Arab world and pan-Arab issues; possible Ba'thi leanings; centered on Graduates Society)
3	Kuwaiti Nationalists (principally concerned with issues affecting Kuwait and Kuwaiti citizens)
3	Social Reform Society (Jami'at al-Islah al-Ijtima'i; Sunni Islamics aligned with Muslim Brotherhood)
2	Heritage Revival Society (Jami' Ihya' al-Turath; Sunni Islamics aligned with al-Salafiya movement)
1	Social Cultural Society (al-Jami'a al-Thiqafiya al-Ijtima'iya; Shi'i Islamics)
Total: 65	50 elected; 15 ex officio

Source: Interviews in Kuwait.

present more attractive candidates in their districts, but it also gives rise to the possibility that tribalist members of future assemblies may be more independent and less willing to support the government automatically.

Four unofficial groupings boasted readily identifiable organizations and put forward candidates for election on established platforms. The most organized of all was the

Democratic Bloc, which ran on a platform emphasizing government inefficiency and the need for administrative reform. It is led by Dr. Ahmad al-Khatib, who was joined in the Sixth Assembly by two colleagues: Sami al-Munayyis, a relative of Muhammad al-Munayyis (the only individual executed as a result of the 1938 events), who serves as editor of the leftist journal, *al-Tali'a*, and Dr. Ahmad al-Rab'i, widely considered to be a Marxist with a background of involvement with leftist groups in the Gulf, who has a Ph.D. in Islamic philosophy from Harvard University and is perhaps the most articulate speaker among the assembly's opposition. One of the more intriguing members of the assembly was Dr. 'Abdullah Fahd al-Nafisi, a controversial former professor at Kuwait University who was defeated in his 1981 bid for election under the Democratic Bloc banner and then spent the intervening years in England and the UAE. His successful campaign in 1985 was based on his sympathy with, though not formal membership in, the Social Reform Society.

Neither the Social Reform Society (leaning toward the Muslim Brotherhood) nor the Social Cultural Society (Shi'i Islamic) did particularly well. The Social Reform Society managed to return two candidates, but this figure was matched by the more conservative Heritage Revival Society (leaning toward the *al-Salafiya* Islamic reform movement). The Social Cultural Society saw its representation drop from two to one. The Islamics' potential influence was considerably greater than their meager number of representatives in the National Assembly would indicate (five members affiliated to these groups, or six including al-Nafisi), given the growing conservative climate in Kuwait and concern over the Iranian revolution and the course of the Iran-Iraq war.[37] Nevertheless, their potential was vitiated by a lack of organization between the groups, differing goals between the Sunnis and Shi'a, and an absence of coordination with other members on common goals.

Two elected members were picked to serve as members of the cabinet (at least one is required under the constitution). Jasim Muhammad al-Khurafi was a persistent critic of the government's economic policy in previous assemblies, as well as a technocrat and social conservative (who appeared to have received the endorsement of the Reform Society in his election campaign). Initially considered a front-runner to replace Muhammad al-'Adsani as speaker, al-Khurafi was picked as minister of finance and economy and soon found himself the target of criticism for economic policies similar to those he had criticized earlier. Khalid Jumay'an Salih al-Jumay'an was named minister of social affairs and labor three weeks after the election, when his predecessor resigned over disagreements on the composition of the cabinet. Associated with the opposition in the assembly, one reported reason for al-Jumay'an's selection was his 'Anayza tribal affiliation. As many as five elected members had turned down cabinet portfolios, reportedly including al-Khatib and al-Nafisi.[38]

Principal Issues

In its brief 16-month existence, the Sixth Assembly proved to be as vocal and critical as the Fourth (suspended in 1977). Indeed, there was more to be vocal about. The government was slow in sorting out the Suq al-Manakh mess, and accusations abounded that the delay was aimed at protecting prominent Kuwaitis and even the Al Sabah involved in the crash. In addition, the economic recession gave substance to populist concerns about growing hardships for poor Kuwaitis, the need to cut back on subsidies to Arab frontline states, and increased utility charges and decreased government services. Other prominent issues included the question of open admission for Kuwaiti students to the university, restrictions on granting citizenship, and the fairness in applying conscription. The emergence of a coalition of National Assembly members in an opposition bloc led to the close questioning of some cabinet members and to the forced resignation of Justice Minister Shaykh Salman al-Du'ayj Al Sabah and the near-resignation of Oil Minister Shaykh 'Ali al-Khalifa Al Sabah.

The Second Suspension (1986)

On July 1, 1986, the cabinet offered its resignation and Amir Jabir subsequently suspended the National Assembly on July 3 and severely curtailed freedom of the press.[39] At the same time, the articles of the constitution concerning the assembly's legislative powers and the provision of new elections within 60 days were amended. The timing was significant, coming soon after a fresh spate of bombings and immediately before a scheduled interrogation of several ministers. Signs of the ruling family's apprehension over external pressures and of a growing lack of patience with the boisterous assembly had been evident for quite some time. The amir had warned the assembly in November 1985 of the necessity for practicing a responsible democracy, admonishing the members that "we are living through delicate and sensitive situations both internally and externally and it is [the assembly's] duty to keep this in mind.[40] In announcing the suspension, the amir's decree lamented that

> the country has faced many ordeals and harsh conditions that it has never experienced all at once before. Thus, its security was exposed to fierce external plots, which threatened souls and almost destroyed the resources of this nation and the source of its livelihood. The flames of war raging between its two Muslim neighbors have almost reached its borders and it has faced a strong economic crisis. Instead of pooling efforts and all parties cooperating in order to contain these crises, opinions were divided, and blocs and parties emerged which have led to the shattering of national unity and the interruption of work until the Council of Ministers has become unable to continue its task.[41]

The amir's decision followed upon a combination of worrisome underlying factors and immediate catalysts. Perhaps the most important underlying factor was the pressure arising from the government's continued inactivity in resolving the Suq al-Manakh scandal and the economic recession. Government restrictions on trading on the official stock exchange and an upsurge in repatriated private funds led to the impromptu creation of an unofficial market for trading in the stock of Kuwaiti and other Gulf companies, many of which existed only on paper. Stocks were purchased with postdated checks and these checks were themselves traded at premiums reaching 400 percent before the boom burst. When the economic recession began to hit in 1982, the bottom fell out of this unofficial exchange as outstanding checks were called in and speculators found themselves unable to make payment on checks they had written. The government stepped in belatedly to suspend trading, compensate small traders, and to sort out the chaotic situation. After a thorough accounting, 28,861 checks were discovered with a face value of KD 26.6 billion ($90.8 billion), although the cancelling of cross-debts made the real total somewhat less than $40 billion. More than two-thirds of the total was held by eight or nine major dealers.[42]

The large sums involved made it difficult for the government to simply bail the investors out and assume responsibility for all debts. Attempts made in 1983 and 1984 to settle accounts by fixing settlement prices of the stocks involved and selling off debtors' assets in land and real estate to major Kuwaiti financial institutions was only partially successful, leaving the actual financial status of many businessmen and institutions in a state of limbo. The continued morass contributed to a loss of confidence in the official stock market and a continuing drain on government resources, with estimates of government costs ranging from $7.5 billion to $10.3 billion. Criminal convictions were levied against a few dealers, but other prominent Kuwaitis (including Al Sabah) seemed to get off scot-free. The finance and economy minister's economic report in late 1985 detailed the destructive impact of Suq al-Manakh on local shareholding companies and recommended that many companies should be liquidated or merged; it raised the possibility that shareholders might be bought out by the government at a cost of $725 million.[43]

Nevertheless, debate over settlement of the financial imbroglio and accusations of a government cover-up of the involvement of prominent individuals continued to occupy the National Assembly. Members of the assembly argued that the government had no business bailing out Suq al-Manakh speculators, especially because government resources were strained because of the economic recession, and that the guilty should be declared bankrupt. The opposition forced Justice Minister Shaykh Salman al-Du'ayj Al Sabah to resign in May 1985 after the disclosure that his 14-year-old son had received $4.5 million from the state fund set up to compensate small investors.[44] A second minister from the ruling family came under attack as well. Shaykh 'Ali al-Khalifa al-'Adhbi Al Sabah, oil minister since 1978, had been entrusted with the finance portfolio as well when the long-serving 'Abd al-Latif al-Hamad resigned over the government's handling of the crisis. Even though he gave up the Finance Ministry in 1985, Shaykh 'Ali was singled out for criticism over his handling of Suq al-Manakh (as well as oil policy and personal financial affairs) in the National Assembly and was very nearly pushed into resignation.

An additional underlying factor involved maneuvering within the Al Sabah. In the last several years, the al-Ahmad branch of the ruling family (to which the amir belongs) has been intensifying its attempts to undermine the position of heir apparent Sa'd al-'Abdullah, the leading figure of the opposing al-Salim branch, in hopes of replacing him with the amir's brother and Foreign Minister Sabah al-Ahmad. It is widely believed that the al-Ahmad encouraged attacks within the National Assembly on such liberal proteges of Shaykh Sa'd as Oil Minister 'Ali al-Khalifa al-'Adhbi Al Sabah (nearly forced to resign in 1985), Education Minister Hasan 'Ali al-Ibrahim (dropped from the July 1986 cabinet), and Communications Minister 'Isa Muhammad al-Mazidi (demoted to minister of state for services affairs in the July 1986 cabinet) to embarrass the prime minister. Shaykh Sa'd expressed his displeasure at these developments by prolonging his post-surgery recuperation in England from De-

cember 1985 until after the twenty-fifth National Day cele-
brations in February 1986 and pointedly refused to enter
the National Assembly in its last months.

The immediate spur to the government's action, and its
justification much as in 1976, was the external climate. In
February 1986, the Iran-Iraq war advanced within artillery
distance of Kuwait with Iran's capture of al-Faw Peninsula,
only a few short miles from Kuwait's Bubiyan Island. The
amirate's determination to remain firm in the face of terrorist acts brought no relief from new attacks. On June 17,
1986, sabotage in the country's oil installations produced
three explosions that temporarily crippled Kuwait's oil production.[45] At the same time, the nationalists had been severely critical of the GCC and the GCC security dependence on
the United States, as well as the preponderance of Kuwaiti
investments in the United States. Saudi Arabia was thought
to be particularly vexed at the freewheeling assembly and
presumably pressured the Al Sabah to shut it down.

The assembly opposition seized on the oil installation
bombings to accuse the government of incompetence and
demanded to interrogate the oil minister, Shaykh 'Ali al-
Khalifa Al Sabah, and the interior minister, Shaykh
Nawwaf al-Ahmad Al Sabah (the amir's older brother), as
well as Finance Minister Jasim Muhammad al-Khurafi. The
Al Sabah already had been pushed to the limit with the
ouster of Shaykh Salman al-Du'ayj, the near-ouster and
continued sniping at Shaykh 'Ali, and the crackdown by the
minister of social affairs and labor (an elected assembly
member) on the Kuwait Football Association's corrupt
board, filled with associates of Shaykh Fahd al-Ahmad, the
younger brother of the amir. The heir apparent and prime
minister, Shaykh Sa'd al-'Abdullah, had been particularly
frustrated, and the combined nationalist/Islamics attack on
his protégés, Oil Minister Shaykh 'Ali and Education Minister Hasan 'Ali al-Ibrahim, undermined his position within
the ruling family as well as in the government. In dissolving
the assembly, the amir assailed those who "have pushed
freedom away until it has become chaos" and those who
"turned nationalism into sectarianism."[46]

The second suspension had an air of permanence about it, unlike the earlier one. The government had been unsuccessful in pushing the Fifth National Assembly to adopt constitutional amendments restricting the assembly's powers. There were allegations that the decision to suspend the assembly had been made soon after the election but was postponed until intelligence and security capabilities were ready. Censorship was far more severe than in 1976, and a number of leading journalists were deported. Without the encumbrance of opposition from the assembly, the electoral law was amended to make naturalized citizens ineligible to vote for 30 years after naturalization.[47]

The formation of the new cabinet on July 12, with the replacement of the education minister opposed by the Islamics and the distribution of additional portfolios to technocrats, representatives of established merchant families, and progovernment ex-assembly members, provided further indication that the government considered the suspension permanent and that it would use the cabinet alone to carry out its program, unencumbered by parliamentary harassment. There was talk of appointment of a consultative council, drawn from the ruling family's natural allies in the merchant community and tribes, which could be expected to apply a rubber stamp to government decisions. The gibe was made that Kuwait *sans parlement* was now truly part of the GCC.

Functions and Principal Issues of the National Assembly

Legitimation

Clearly, the idea of popular representation is deeply rooted in Kuwaiti history and there is great pride in "Kuwaiti democracy." Kuwaitis also take pride in the relative openness and give-and-take of their political system relative to those of their GCC neighbors. The right to popular representation, as enshrined in the constitution and as established in the operation of the National Assembly since independence, is not in doubt. Much of the credit is owed to the positive role played by Amir 'Abdullah in establishing the assembly after independence and Amir Jabir's action in ending its suspension in 1981.

The political system rests on the idea, honored perhaps more in constitutional rhetoric than practice, that sovereignty resides in the people and that the amir exercises authority as their agent. Even as the constitution specifies that the system of government is democratic (Art. 6), it stipulates hereditary rulership within the Al Sabah (Art. 4). Although the constitution envisages an indirect popular role in the process of succession through approval of the amir's nominee as heir apparent, it describes this role as *mubaya'a*, which connotes the traditional function of pledging allegiance or fealty rather than equal participation or confirmation (Art. 4). Consequently, it is the exact balance of power between the ruler (and the ruling family) and the citizenry that still remains in doubt. The struggle over this balance defines the extent of true democracy existing in Kuwait.

Reflecting the wider Arab environment, the National Assembly presented a considerably more radical image in the 1960s than in the 1980s. Few Kuwaitis today advocate an end to the monarchy, but liberals and nationalists argue for considerably more power-sharing. In particular, they argue that the offices of heir apparent and prime minister should be decoupled, making the assembly more of a true parliament. Such a change would allow the assembly to apply votes of no-confidence to the prime minister and the cabinet as a whole without provoking a constitutional crisis.

Formalized Majlis

As an elected body (and not appointed as in the consultative councils), the National Assembly bears little resemblance to the traditional *majlis*. Nevertheless, the *diwaniy-*

as held regularly by most assembly members provide a forum in which they may solicit public opinion on issues, as well as receive complaints and requests for assistance. Thus this function of the *diwaniya* represents a transitional phase on the route to a formal political relationship between elected politicians and their constituency. Office suites for all elected members were included in the new assembly complex, but only one member, a strong supporter of the assembly's institutionalization, utilized his assembly office, complete with a full-time secretary, on a regular basis to meet constituents.

Legislative Role

From its inception, the National Assembly has exercised its constitutionally granted right to review and approve legislation.[48] Kuwait's direct and free elections raises the possibility of the emergence of a majority bloc of members opposed to the government. In practice, this has not happened. A vote of two-thirds is necessary to overturn the amir's veto. The cabinet provides an automatic bloc of pro-government votes amounting to around 25 percent of the total. In the Sixth Assembly, the 17 cabinet votes out of the 65 vote total meant the government needed to secure only an additional five votes to block any veto override. As table 3 (page 44) shows, in reality the government could count on receiving a majority on nearly every vote, relying on the tribalist half of the elected membership as well as other progovernment members. Consequently, the government had every expectation of having even routine legislation requiring only a simple majority passed.

The Sixth Assembly, like its predecessors, took its legislative role seriously and forced the government's retreat and/or concessions on a number of issues. The assembly cited financial stringencies in officially terminating subsidies of approximately KD100 million ($340 million) to Arab frontline states and the Palestine Liberation Organization (PLO). The government objected strenuously to the action, but appeared to secure an understanding that subventions would be maintained by diversions from an enlarged aid package.[49] Perhaps most shocking was the assembly's role in banning alcohol from the amirate in early 1984. Although the government had no desire to confront either the assembly or the country's conservative mood, the amir reluctantly vetoed the law because of its application to non-Muslims and embassies as well as Kuwaitis. For the first time ever, the assembly overrode the veto. This was clearly a special issue, however, and the government, recognizing the dangers of appearing to be on the wrong side of Islamic strictures, made no attempt to round up favorable votes.[50]

Government Accountability

The Sixth Assembly brought the issue to the test when its constitutional right to express no-confidence in cabinet ministers was applied to two Al Sabah ministers. The constitutional issue was narrowly avoided when Justice Minister Shaykh Salman resigned on the eve of a no-confidence vote, but the assembly's muscle-flexing in spring 1985 clearly alarmed the regime and was a principal factor in the July 1986 dissolution, only days before several additional ministers were scheduled for similar treatment. Although tactically the Sixth Assembly may have gone too far too quickly in testing the regime on this issue, it appeared to have firmly implanted the acceptance of its right to participate in the making of financial and oil policy as had earlier assemblies.

The decline in oil revenues, downstream diversification of the oil sector, deepening economic recession, and Suq al-Manakh all provided grist for the robust debate over government policy during the Sixth Assembly. The government's economic report of December 1985, with its proposed use of state funds to buy out ailing companies and put Suq al-Manakh to rest, came under sharp criticism. Specifically, objections were raised to the extent of government majority ownership of companies, given its existing large or majority holdings in the banking, investment, in-surance, industrial, and service sectors. The use of nearly $1.2 billion of public funds, on top of the billions already spent, was attacked as a waste of money on an enterprise that would not help to revive the economy. Others claimed that the government was bowing to the interest of wealthy and influential Kuwaitis and ignoring the small debtors who had no influence.[51]

Shaykh Salman's timely resignation and dissolution of the Sixth Assembly averted a potentially traumatic con-frontation over whether Al Sabah members of the cabinet were as accountable as other ministers to the National As-sembly in practice as well as constitutional stipulation. But as long as the ruling family occupies some cabinet posts and the National Assembly is in operation, public scrutiny and criticism of the Al Sabah ministers' activities is inevita-ble. The dilemma can be avoided either by doing away with the assembly permanently or by rewriting the constitution to recreate the assembly as a consultative council; neither course is likely to be a wise one in the long run. A more reasonable or logical solution would be to leave Al Sabah out of the cabinet altogether. Indeed, the numbers of family members in cabinets formed since the National Assembly was formed has steadily declined, from 11 in January 1963 and 9 in March 1964 to 6 in March 1985 and July 1986.[52] Jordan and Morocco provide a precedent within the Middle East for the exclusion of members of the ruling family from the cabinet.

Kuwait, however, is unlikely to adopt this practice in the foreseeable future for two major reasons. Nearly all the ruling families of the GCC prefer to retain direct control of new and untested bureaucratic institutions, particularly de-fense, interior, foreign affairs, and information; the office of prime minister is filled by either the ruler or the heir appar-ent in all six countries (the ruler of Dubai serves as the UAE's prime minister). Furthermore, the Gulf's ruling houses consist of extended clans, numbering in the thou-sands in the case of Saudi Arabia, Bahrain, and Qatar, rather than closely related families as elsewhere. Ministerial portfolios are a major tool in achieving a viable balance of intra-family interests.

Incipient Populism

It is not surprising that most elected assembly members should pose as "champions of the people" in a system of direct elections in small districts. Because of the small number of Kuwaiti nationals, candidates tend to be personally acquainted with most fellow citizens. And, because of the small size of the electoral districts (consisting of only several thousand voters) and the lavish expenditure on campaigns, candidates have ample opportunity for face-to-face contact with nearly every potential voter.

Apart from its socializing and opinion-gathering functions, the institution of the *diwaniya* reinforces the populist role of the assembly member. Constituents often attend *diwaniyas* to petition the member or gain his assistance in a personal matter, in much the same way they might approach the ruler or a minister or governor. Although the member may settle the request for assistance by using his position and influence to find the constituent a job or get him a loan, for example, petitions may be taken to the assembly's committee on petitions and complaints or to the full assembly for discussion.[53] The mechanism of petitions provides members with an ideal justification to speak out in assembly debates, especially to "play to the galleries," where the audience may number as many as a thousand, as well as to the extensive newspaper coverage of assembly sessions.

During the Sixth Assembly, instances of populist appeals appeared during the proposal to increase utility charges and the university's admission policy. In deciding to raise the cost of electricity, health care, and traffic department services, the government cited the need to avoid cutting into state reserves and claimed its actions were directed against people who left their air conditioners on when they went away for the summer. Opponents spoke of the adverse impact on poor Kuwaitis, pointed out that Iraq had not raised its electricity charges despite six years of war, and suggested that the government could more profitably look elsewhere to cut costs, such as an overmanned civil service and foreign aid to undeserving countries.[54]

Similarly, bedouin members attacked the minister of education and the Kuwait University administration for refusing admission to some Kuwaiti students. Opponents disputed the university's claim of maintaining academic standards and called for a return to an open admissions policy for Kuwaitis, arguing that rejected Kuwaiti students should have priority over the one-third of the student body consisting of foreign students.[55] All told, the assembly was a particularly popular institution, with ordinary sessions attracting audiences of up to a thousand spectators.

At times, the rhetoric of assembly debate and statements to the media gave the impression that nearly all elected assembly members fell into the ranks of opposition. Even the tribalist members, staunch supporters of the regime, tended to start off assembly sessions with declarations of the government's neglect of their constituencies' educational, transport, and social services needs. These criticisms did not affect their voting patterns, however.

Women's Right to Vote

Women's suffrage has long been debated in Kuwait.[56] Lu'lu'a Qattami, head of the Women's Cultural and Social Society since 1966, has been at the forefront of the right-to-vote campaign. She has noted that Kuwaiti women participate in voting for the councils that head the cooperative societies in Kuwait City's 57 districts, as well as the councils for the country's 42 social or cultural societies. Furthermore, women students at Kuwait University are very active in student politics and even vote and hold office in the student society – but of course they have not been able to vote after leaving the university.

Opinions run strong on both sides of the issue, and

there is considerable resistance to women's voting rights. In October 1984, leaflets containing a *fatwa* (religious finding) against coeducation in Kuwait by a Saudi *'alim* (religious leader) were distributed outside mosques. The incident set off a furor in Kuwait and pitted liberals against Islamics. The latter might be expected to oppose the issue, as they indeed did in blocking a 1982 bill, but a Kuwaiti *fatwa* against women voting was opposed in the 1985 National Assembly by a combination of Islamics, including the Social Reform Society (Muslim Brotherhood), and liberals. But opposition can be broader. A 1985 poll of men eligible to vote showed that 58 percent opposed electoral rights for women and only 27 percent were in favor. Similar attitudes are widespread among male and even female university students.

The voting-rights campaign was given an enormous boost by Heir Apparent and Prime Minister Shaykh Sa'd al-'Abdullah's statement in 1980 that the "time has come to take note of the position of the Kuwaiti woman and her effective role in society and to put forward the matter of the vote for study and discussion." The amir is also said to be on record favoring women voting, but, typical of divisions in Kuwaiti society, the heir apparent's wife, Shaykha Latifa, has come out against it, saying few women involved in political activities "have the necessary understanding in this regard."

A majority of women are still either indifferent or actively against the idea. When Qattami led a group of women to the National Assembly in January 1982 to push for the inclusion of the issue on its agenda, a better organized countermovement sprang up among Kuwaiti women opposing their right to vote. Women's groups have stopped pushing the issue, in part perhaps because of the circulation of a petition signed by 1,000 women at the time of the 1985 election, contending that female suffrage was incompatible with Islam.

Attempts have been made to lobby the National Assembly to take action since 1971, when the Society for the Advancement of the Family, Kuwait's first women's association, presented a petition to the assembly. A bill that would give women the vote but exclude them from office was introduced in the 1981 assembly and was blocked by Islamics the following year. On February 11, 1984, Kuwaiti women activists initiated a legal battle against the government, charging that the denial of their right to vote was a violation of the constitutional guarantees of democracy and the equality of all citizens and represented sexual discrimination, forbidden under the constitution. At that time, three leading members of the women's movement attempted to get their names included on the electoral roll but were rejected by officials at election registration offices. Another 13 women tried a similar move soon after. While all 13 were rejected, 8 did manage to report the rejection to the police.

During the 1985 election campaign, women's groups induced several candidates of the liberal/nationalist bloc to declare their intention to work for female suffrage if elected, although there was grumbling later that some of the elected candidates ignored their campaign promises. Nevertheless, after the election, a group of deputies brought forward a bill to grant women the vote. The assembly's Internal Affairs Committee, three of whose five members were implacable foes of women's suffrage, called on the Ministry of Awqaf and Islamic Affairs to rule on its validity. The ministry issued a *fatwa* declaring that "the nature of the electoral process befits men, who are endowed with ability and expertise: it is not permissible that women recommend or nominate other women or men." The committee consistently tabled the measure until the assembly was suspended.

The potential impact of women voters is considerable. Women could form a majority of voters because they constitute about 52 percent of Kuwaiti citizens. Liberal women voters probably would be in the minority. Most women voters from tribes or conservative backgrounds undoubtedly would support tribalists or Islamics for election, and the argument could be made to conservative assembly members that giving women the vote would serve their interests.

If the assembly had not been suspended, a plausible scenario might have had the issue of women's suffrage brought up again in the Seventh Session (to have been elected in 1989), possibly with a more favorably constituted committee that could have allowed a bill on the floor. Even if not passed in that session, the resulting debate and attention conceivably could have spurred the subsequent Eighth Session to pass a women's right-to-vote bill, thereby giving women the right to vote in the elections for the Ninth Session (1997). The issue of women's equality, furthest advanced in Kuwait among the Gulf states, is currently stalled, however, given the retraction of voting rights for men and the growing conservative climate.

Prospects for Reinstitution
of the National Assembly

The harshness of the action and the disregard for the constitution, in what is undoubtedly the most constitution-conscious state in the Gulf, places the future of Kuwaiti democracy in grave doubt. Of all the GCC states, Kuwait indisputably has traveled the furthest along the path of political change and the reimposition of authoritarian rule is not well tolerated by sophisticated Kuwaitis, aware of both Western precepts of democracy and antecedents within Kuwait.

Although the deteriorating position of Iraq in its long-running war with Iran has diverted Kuwaitis' attention from the assembly's short-term disappearance, a lengthy period of suspension is likely to provoke serious and fundamental internal tensions. A functioning assembly helps to create habits of cooperation between sectarian and ethnic communities and provides a forum for public discussion of areas of tension and disagreement. Its continued suspen-

sion is likely to contribute to increased polarization between Sunnis and the Shi'a. The history of Kuwaiti aspirations for popular representation over the course of the twentieth century suggests that agitation for the assembly's
return is probable. The absence of the assembly only prevents the airing of serious and constructive debate on the
direction of future economic change and development.

3

Bahrain

Bahrain was the second state in the Gulf to create an elected parliament but the first to suspend it. The brief, troubled existence of the National Assembly (*al-Majlis al-Watani*, 1973–1975) seemed to reconfirm the regime's fears of providing a forum for radical, leftist opposition to the government. Although there has been steady popular sympathy for the reconstitution of the assembly, such support has not as yet intensified into a demand, and the government, bolstered by the opposition of a number of prominent members of the ruling family, has seen fit to leave the issue in abeyance indefinitely.

The Bahraini political system displays significant differences from Kuwait because of its historical development. The origins of the Al Khalifa are similar to the Al Sabah, particularly as the two clans come from the same 'Anayza tribal confederation and migrated together from central Arabia to the shores of the Gulf. After reaching Zubara in the Qatar peninsula in the eighteenth century, their paths diverged. While the Al Sabah moved north along the mainland to settle in Kuwait, the Al Khalifa along with their tribal allies from the 'Utub took advantage of the disintegration of Persian control over Bahrain to seize control of the islands in about 1782. In effect, the Sunni Arab tribesmen replaced the Persian empire as overlords of the largely Shiʻi Baharna inhabitants of the islands.[1]

Bahraini society is divided into four principal groups. The Bahrainis of Sunni Arab tribal origin form the traditional aristocracy, centered on the ruling Al Khalifa and their tribal allies, including both tribes that accompanied the Al Khalifa on their invasion of the islands and tribes that arrived later (prominent names include al-Nuʻaymi, al-Rumayhi, ʻAskar, Al Bin ʻAli, al-Manaʻina, al-Dawasir, al-Jalahima, al-Sulayti, and al-Musallim). The Sunni *hawala* come next in social rank, being families of Arab origin who migrated to the Persian side of the Gulf in the far past and then have entered Bahrain at various periods in the last several centuries (notable families include Fakhru, Kanu, al-Muʼayyad, Matar, and al-ʻAwadi).

The Shiʻa majority of the population (constituting between 55 percent and 70 percent of all Bahrainis) are divided into the Baharna and the ʻAjam (or Persians). Although some of the latter have been in Bahrain since the seventeenth century (and accepted Bahraini citizenship in 1937), many have immigrated to the islands during the twentieth century. The Baharna are far more numerous, are concentrated in the rural villages, and are thought to be the descendants of the original inhabitants. The distinctions between Sunni and Shiʻa, urban and rural, well-to-do and poor provide Bahrain with a relatively greater sense of social stratification than its neighbors and have provoked economic and political tensions.

Bahrain was the first oil state in the Gulf outside of Iran and Iraq. Oil was first discovered in Bahrain in 1932, first exported in 1934, and a refinery was built in 1937. As a consequence, Bahrain experienced significant socioeconomic change related to an oil-fed economy decades before Kuwait and Saudi Arabia and even longer before the lower Gulf states. The depletion of its reserves makes it the first Gulf state to enter a post-oil era. In addition, Bahrain's reputation as a regional entrepôt and cosmopolitan center antedated oil. Because of its oil industry, labor organization and disputes appeared at an early date. The combination of an industrial workforce and the sometimes repressive nature of Al Khalifa rule have produced a politicized opposition to the regime.

Background

Bahraini politics in the twentieth century largely has been the preserve of the Al Khalifa, their tribal allies, and a few prominent merchants. The privileges and authority of the Al Khalifa were virtually unchallenged before significant reforms were introduced in the 1920s at British insistence. These reforms included reorganization of the customs, courts, and *awqaf*; improvements in land surveys, public works, education, and pearling regulations; the establishment of a municipality and police force; and the appointment of a British adviser. Although these reforms prevented the worst of frequent abuses by members of the Al Khalifa and other shaykhs, they did not eliminate legitimate economic and political grievances.

As a consequence, protests and clashes cropped up among the Shi'a (1922), students (1928), pearl divers (1932), the Shi'a (1934, 1935), between Persian and Baharna Shi'a (1942), and Bahrain Petroleum Company (BAPCO) employees in 1938, 1942, 1948, and 1965. Although earlier protests tended to be prompted by either the merchant community's opposition to British influence or Shi'i reaction to injustices, gradually the sectarian nature of these protests became infused with nationalism and they were transformed into sustained political struggles vis-à-vis the regime, accompanied by undertones of ideological dissension. Movements directed against the internal policies and the state's British connection erupted in 1921–1923, 1934–1935, 1938, 1947–1948, 1953–1956, and 1965.[2]

The British-imposed abdication in 1923 of Shaykh 'Isa ibn 'Ali in favor of his son Hamad was opposed by both conservative elements and embryonic Bahraini nationalists (exclusively Sunni), led by 'Abd al-Wahhab al-Zayyani. They convened a "Bahrain National Congress" in 1923 to formulate a list of demands, including the noninterference of Britain in internal affairs and the establishment of a consultative council. The demands were presented to the British who had al-Zayyani and several others deported to India a few months later. While British-instituted reforms continued to take root during the remainder of the decade, particularly under the guidance of the British adviser (Charles Belgrave, who was virtually a one-man administration), grievances against the Al Khalifa and Sunni establishment remained.

A delegation of leading Shi'a presented a list of demands to Shaykh Hamad and Belgrave in 1934, which included codification of the law and proportional representation on the Municipal Councils (established in Manama in 1920 and Muharraq in 1927 as partly nominated and partly elected bodies) and the Educational Council. Failing to receive satisfaction from the government, they approached the Political Agent, who maintained he had no jurisdiction in internal affairs. There the matter rested, although it was not forgotten.

The Constitutional Movement of 1938

Many of the same elements that had provoked political agitation in Kuwait in 1938 were present also in Bahrain. Grievances remained against intolerant members of the ruling family, increased education and communications produced a fertile environment for the dissemination of Arab nationalist sentiment (particularly from Iraq), and the introduction of oil revenues raised expectations as well as concern over their equitable distribution. There was also a group of emerging well-to-do merchants who, like their counterparts in Kuwait, sought a greater say in state policies. As had happened in Kuwait, these merchants sought an ally in Shaykh Hamad's son Salman, who had not yet been named heir apparent but feared the possibility of his uncle 'Abdullah being elected by the family in the event of

Shaykh Hamad's sudden death. One merchant, Yusuf Fakhru, took it upon himself to gather the other merchants together with Shaykh Salman and some Shi'a representatives to formulate a list of demands, including clarification of Shaykh Salman's position, the establishment of a legislative council, and further reforms within the state administration.

Graffiti and posters in support of these demands and against Belgrave began to appear in October 1938. The adviser sought to defuse the situation by correcting some of the problems in the administration and courts. A separate overture was made to the Shi'a, to divorce them from the Sunni elements, and the government arrested a number of Sunni leaders of the movement in November. This resulted in more posters, demonstrations, preparation for a strike against BAPCO, and a call for a general strike, which soon collapsed for lack of leadership. The more moderate elements immediately formed a committee to draw up more reasonable demands, covering improvements in education, the courts, the municipalities, and the formation of a labor committee and a consultative council. The amir rejected the majority of these demands, including the consultative council, and BAPCO subsequently dismissed 18 leaders of the strike. Two leaders of the movement, Sa'd al-Shamlan and Ahmad al-Shirawi, were exiled to India. Political grievances went underground again, to resurface later.

Radicalization and Repression in the 1950s and 1960s

The decade and a half following the 1938 events saw a deepening politicization, particularly through the development of social and cultural clubs and the founding of a local press. Students abroad, exposed to pan-Arab nationalist and socialist movements, returned home and founded cultural/political clubs, displacing an earlier generation of more conservative opposition leaders. Prominent among these were 'Abd al-Rahman al-Bakir and 'Abd al-'Aziz al-

Shamlan (whose father had been a leader of the 1938 events). Eventually, an alliance was struck between Sunni and Shi'i activists against a regime perceived as fundamentally intolerant to both sects.

Strikes broke out against BAPCO in 1942–1943 and again in 1947–1948, when they coincided with demonstrations against British policy in Palestine. Revolutionary Egypt under Nasser replaced monarchical Iraq under the Hashimis as the formative influence in Bahraini political thought, and the paternalistic attitude of Belgrave no longer seemed so benevolent to many Bahrainis. Changing expectations of government due to socioeconomic development, the growth of Arab nationalist sentiment among Bahrainis, and mounting anti-British feelings all played a part in maintaining a climate of hostility between the regime and a core of political activists.

A series of Sunni-Shi'a incidents in 1953 and 1954 culminated in violence, the killing of four Shi'a by the police, and a general strike in July 1954. Several months later, 'Abd al-Rahman al-Bakir, returning from a short period of exile, was threatened with the loss of his passport and citizenship for organizing a taxi-drivers cooperative. A small group of like-minded activists gathered together sympathizers from among both the Sunnis and Shi'a in a congress to defend al-Bakir and to work against the Belgrave "dictatorship." As a consequence, the Higher Executive Committee (HEC—al-Hay'a al-Tanfidhiya al-'Ulya) was formed on October 13, 1954, which petitioned the government for a legislative council, the codification of criminal and civil law, the right to form trade unions, and the establishment of a higher appeal court.

The government initially rejected the demands but then entered into negotiations with the committee. A week-long general strike in December forced the government to appoint a seven-man advisory committee to investigate matters regarding education, public health, judicial affairs, and public security (and to ensure better treatment of the Shi'a by the police and in the courts). A labor committee, composed of elected BAPCO workers, company representatives, and government officials was established in April 1955.

In September 1955, the ruler was persuaded to discuss the general question of reforms, for which the HEC had been pressing for more than a year. By October, the negotiations had proceeded to the point that the ruler agreed to set up three councils, half elected and half appointed, to supervise the departments of health and education and various municipalities. Not incidentally, as it provided the people of Bahrain with some say in their government, it also served to sidetrack, at least temporarily, the HEC's demands for a legislative council, as well as objections to the adviser. The election for the Education Committee was held on February 10, 1955, with 19,000 votes cast out of an electorate of 23,000 males above the age of 18. All six HEC candidates swept the balloting, humiliating the government-favored candidates from the conservative National Front. The election for the Health Council on April 23 had the same result; the municipalities council was never elected. Neither elected council functioned, however, because of disputes over the appointment of their chairmen and the failure of continuing negotiations.

Tensions and fitful bargaining between the government and a divided HEC continued through 1955 into 1956. A few days after the mobbing of the car of British Foreign Secretary Selwyn Lloyd in March 1956, the police killed three people during an altercation in the market, and riots ensued.[3] The HEC responded with another general strike and renewed its demands for a legislative council, the codification of the law, and the ouster of Belgrave, as well as an inquiry into the market deaths. A compromise was reached, by which the committee dropped its demands for the council and Belgrave's ouster, al-Bakir stepped down as the HEC's secretary general and left the country, and the committee agreed to change its name.[4] A 10-man Administrative Council was formed to take part of the burden off Belgrave and to deal with public complaints, but it was regarded with suspicion as seven members were from the Al Khalifa.[5] The strike was lifted and the government recognized the newly named Committee for National Unity (CNU – *hay'at al-ittihad al-watani*), with 'Abd al-'Aziz al-Shamlan as secretary general.

A long series of ineffective negotiations between the CNU and the government – with the British Political Agency in Bahrain serving as the intermediary – led nowhere, and the CNU eventually broke them off and, despite deep divisions, defiantly established its own paramilitary force. The situation remained deceptively calm despite mass meetings and a demonstration in support of 'Abd al-Rahman al-Bakir on his return from abroad. But riots broke out after Israel's invasion of Suez on October 29, 1956, and the CNU issued a statement condemning the British and French for their participation. A protest march organized by the CNU got out of hand, and a mob burned down the BOAC staff flats at Muharraq and attacked British businesses, the Roman Catholic church, *al-Khalij* newspaper offices, and the government's Public Works Department. On November 6, in the midst of a general strike, al-Bakir, al-Shamlan, 'Abd 'Ali al-'Ulaywat, and two other leaders of the CNU were arrested, the committee was declared illegal, and the press was suspended under a "state of emergency" law.

The ruler first proposed that the leaders be banished for up to 10 years, preferably to England or a British possession. The British expressed reluctance, particularly as the men had not been accused of any crime, and Whitehall suggested that a conviction for treason would make drafting the necessary legislation easier.[6] As a consequence, the five prisoners were placed on trial on December 23, 1956 in the village of al-Budayya', the nearest point to the island prison where they had been held. Because they refused to recognize the legality of the proceedings and were not provided with defense counsel, the trial was over in a day or two, and all five defendants were found guilty by the three Al Khalifa judges of plotting to murder the ruler, to overthrow the government, and inciting violence during the November 2 procession. Al-Bakir, al-Shamlan, and al-'Ulaywat were sentenced to 14 years imprisonment and taken immediately by a British warship to the Atlantic island of St. Helena, where they remained until 1961. The other two defendants received 10-year terms, and both served nine years on the Bahraini prison island of Jidda.[7]

Active political agitation against the regime collapsed with the demise of the CNU and the flight of a number of its supporters to neighboring countries. The reinforced and British-supervised police and security forces gradually assumed increasing importance, particularly with the retirement of Belgrave in 1957.

From then until independence, political opposition necessarily had to operate underground. It is arguable that the regime's repression discredited moderation and forced a turn to radicalism as the only viable alternative. The Arab Nationalists' Movement, Ba'th Party, and Marxist groups all were able to recruit Bahraini students abroad and form cells within Bahrain. A demonstration against BAPCO evolved into a general strike organized by leftist groups under the National Front banner in March 1965. The confrontation turned into violence and a number of demonstrators were killed before the government was able to regain control.

The Constitutional Assembly

In 1968, the British government announced it would withdraw officially in 1971 from its legally paramount position in the Gulf. The imminent independence of the various statelets still under British protection prodded the rulers of Bahrain, Qatar, and the Trucial Coast (later the United Arab Emirates) into negotiations over unity in a single state. Despite a promising start, the negotiations floundered and Bahrain and Qatar went their separate ways.

As a consequence, by 1970 it became clear that Bahrain's impending status as a separate sovereign state required major improvements in the structure of government. Government departments had been added in the 1950s and 1960s but executive authority still was held informally by the Al Khalifa, the Administrative Council notwithstanding. Although partially elected municipal councils existed in the country's urban centers, the largely Shi'i rural areas were still administered by local officials (*mukhtars*) appointed by the ruler. On January 19, 1970, the Administrative Council was transformed into a Council of State, serving as a de facto cabinet and composed of a combination of Al Khalifa and notables close to the regime. This council was retermed the Council of Ministers upon independence in 1971.[8]

The Constituent Assembly and the Constitution

Following workers' riots against the spiraling cost of living in March 1972, Shaykh 'Isa initiated consultations on the subject of a constitution and national assembly.[9] On July 20, 1972, the ruler announced elections for a Constituent Assembly to approve a draft constitution to be drawn up by a government subcommittee (i.e., by the Al Khalifa family). In the elections, held on December 1, 1972, 22 members were chosen out of 58 candidates by 27,000 male voters. The ruler appointed an additional eight members and the total membership swelled to 42 by the inclusion of the 12-member cabinet as ex officio members.

While the leftist National Liberation Front of Bahrain (NLFB, formed in 1955) and the Bahraini branch of the Popular Front for the Liberation of Oman and the Arabian Gulf (PFLOAG, then waging rebellion in Oman's Dhufar province) boycotted the elections, 10 of the elected members came from leaders of the nationalist or reformist movement, many of whom had been exiled in the 1950s. Many votes were cast on a sectarian basis, particularly among the Shi'a who tended to elect conservative candidates. Fourteen of the 22 elected members were Shi'a. A prominent businessman, Ibrahim al-Urayyad, was elected president of the assembly, but 'Abd al-'Aziz al-Shamlan, who had spent more than four years in exile on St. Helena, was chosen as the assembly's vice president.[10] The denial of voting rights to women provoked Bahrain's women's societies to organize meetings in August and September 1972 to protest their exclusion, and a petition demanding the right to participate in the political life of the country was presented to the amir on November 20, 1972. It had no effect.[11]

The bloc patterns of the assembly virtually assured the passage of the constitution without major changes. The government could count on the votes of its ministers and generally those of the appointed members, mostly prosperous merchants and businessmen. The conservative bloc, representing rural districts, viewed the process from an almost exclusively Shi'a perspective, while the reformists were deeply divided among themselves, thus vitiating their ability to enact favorable changes in the document. After six months of vigorous debate, on June 2, 1973 the assembly approved a constitution largely modeled on that of Kuwait.[12] In fact, Kuwait's constitutional expert was delegated to Bahrain to help write the constitution and the electoral law. The latter, almost an exact replica of the Kuwaiti law, set the voting age at 20, effectively denied naturalized citizens the right to vote because they were required to have been naturalized for 10 years prior to the enactment of the 1963 citizenship law, and prohibited women and members of the armed forces and police from voting.[13]

Although the Bahraini constitution, like that of Kuwait, defined the country as a hereditary monarchy, it specified that succession should fall to Shaykh 'Isa's eldest son and then to his eldest son in perpetuity (Art. 1).[14] The constitution provides for the separation of legislative, executive, and judicial powers, and vests legislative power jointly in the amir and the National Assembly (Art. 32). Like Kuwait, Bahrain is not a true parliamentary state, as the amir has the sole power to appoint and remove the prime minister and the other members of the cabinet (Art. 33). Unlike Kuwait, the government is not bound to take any elected members of the assembly into the cabinet, although it may do so in assemblies after the first; ministers are to be ex officio members of the assembly and their number is limited to 14 (Art. 33).

The amir alone is given the right to initiate, as well as ratify and promulgate, laws. A law is considered ratified if the amir does not return it to the assembly for reconsideration within 30 days; if it is returned (i.e., vetoed), the assembly may override the veto by a simple majority (Art. 35). The National Assembly is to consist of 30 members elected by secret ballot in the first assembly and 40 members thereafter, as well as the ministers (Art. 43), and the term is four years (Art. 45). Members must be Bahraini citizens, 30 years old, and literate in Arabic (Art. 44). The amir may dissolve the assembly once but must call for new elections within two months, failing which the assembly is restored (Art. 65).

Ministers are responsible to the National Assembly for the affairs of their respective ministries, and assembly members have the right to put questions to individual ministers (and the prime minister) on matters within their competence and to pass votes of no-confidence against individual ministers (Arts. 66–68). Votes of no-confidence can be raised against the prime minister only if he holds a specific portfolio; if two-thirds of the assembly decide they cannot cooperate with the prime minister, the matter is submitted to the amir, who may relieve the prime minister of office and appoint a new cabinet or dissolve the assembly (Art. 69).

Individual members of the assembly have the right to initiate bills, and a minimum of five members may raise discussion on any subject of general interest (Arts. 71–72). Membership in the National Assembly is deemed incompatible with public office except in the case of ministers (Art. 80). The annual budget must be ratified by the National Assembly (Art. 94), and a two-thirds majority and the approval of the amir is required for revision of the constitution, except that the principle of hereditary rule may not be proposed for amendment (Art. 104).

The Brief Existence of the National Assembly (1973–1975)

The Election and Membership[15]

The first elections were held on December 7, 1973, with 114 candidates vying for about 29,000 votes for the 30 seats. Sixteen of the winning candidates were Shi'a, seven had one or more university degrees (including one Ph.D.), and the average age was 37. Officially, all the candidates were independents, but the "popular" (leftist, nationalist, or reformist) bloc won eight seats and the "religious conservative" bloc won six seats. Many of the "popular" candidates had taken part in the labor-student strikes of 1965 in which some were arrested and/or imprisoned. The NLFB took part in the elections while the PFLOAG abstained again.

The winning "popular" candidates included four Arab nationalists, two Marxists, one socialist, and one Ba'thi.[16] Their ranks included both Sunnis and Shi'a, including one Shi'a elected from a predominantly Sunni district. This group held views similar to those of Ahmad al-Khatib's Democratic Bloc in Kuwait, and there was some cooperation between the two blocs. Their platform was dedicated to deepening the process and institutionalization of democracy, giving women the right to vote, establishing a Bahraini university and reforming the educational system to eradicate links to the colonial past, and moving Bahrain to nonalignment between East and West with closer links to Arab issues.[17]

Not surprisingly, the "religious conservative" bloc was diametrically opposed to the "popular" bloc in ideological terms. Less of an organized group than the "popular" bloc, the roots of the "religious" bloc were among the religious leaders and traditionalists in the rural Shi'a areas. All six winning religious candidates were Shi'a. Two of these were jurists, one was a journalist, one was a *mulla*, and two were elementary school teachers.[18] Once in office, the six independently elected candidates formed a bloc around a platform focusing on enforcing conformity with Islamic precepts, such as prohibiting alcohol, coeducation, and the participation of women in public life.

The remaining 16 victorious candidates were independent of either bloc and ideologically diverse. Their ranks included merchants, contractors, a pharmacist, and a real estate dealer. Although most belonged to prominent merchant families, some were self-made but wealthy men.[19] The nationalists regarded them as liberals, representing the bourgeoisie; the "liberals" were seen as being for free trade, while the nationalists were for industrialization and trade unions. Three had been political activists in the 1950s and two were thought to be Arab nationalists but had remained aloof from the "popular" bloc as a result of family pressure. In addition, one member of the Al Khalifa ran for office, against the wishes of the ruling family, and was elected, becoming known as the "red shaykh" because of his supposed leftist beliefs. Several unsuccessful candidates were given ministerial posts to maintain a favorable sectarian and political balance.

Issues and Activities

The functioning of the National Assembly in its first year was characterized by trial and error. Rather than participate in the drafting of laws, the assembly found itself relegated to discussing proposed laws already drafted by the government or projects already under way. Much of its time was taken up by discussion of petitions from individuals and groups. The independents came to be regarded as the "government bloc" because they tended to support government policy in general, while the "popular" and "religious" blocs formed a tacit alliance against the government on various issues.

The strength and demands of the vocal "popular" bloc — including the nationalization of banks, the oil companies, and refineries, and an end to the U.S. presence in Bahrain — prevented the government from pushing through legisla-

tion without lengthy debate and substantive changes. The composition and activities of the assembly clearly worried many within the Al Khalifa (a large proportion of whom had never approved of the assembly in the first place), and, as in the case of Kuwait, there were allegations of Saudi (as well as Iranian and U.S.) pressure to end the dangerous experiment altogether.

The Security Law and Dissolution

Following labor riots in January and June of 1974, the amir sought to enact a new security law without recourse to the assembly. It would give the Ministry of the Interior the authority to arrest and detain for three years without a court appearance anyone suspected of working against the state or even intending to act.[20] The "popular" bloc, with support from other members, demanded that the law be submitted to the assembly and debated there; the government, uncertain of how the voting would go, prevaricated.

Over the ensuing months, the issue received considerable public attention and revived concerns over a return to the government policy and activities of the 1950s and 1960s, with its "state of emergency." The government's position weakened as the issue remained in the public consciousness and debates continued in the National Assembly. Many of the independents were swayed by public opinion to oppose the law, and the "popular" bloc gained the "religious" bloc's support against the law in return for its backing of such issues as the prohibition of treatment of female patients by male doctors and women's photographs on identity cards.

Sensing defeat, the government withdrew from participation in the assembly in May 1975, forcing an adjournment. It apparently hoped that a compromise could be reached over the summer but none appeared. On August 23, 1975, the Interior Ministry announced the arrest of 30 NFLB and PFLOAG members and banned activities of the Union of Bahraini Students. The prime minister (Shaykh

Khalifa ibn Salman Al Khalifa, the amir's brother) charged that it was impossible to work with the assembly, submitted his resignation the next day, and, on the following day, formed a new cabinet. The amir dissolved the National Assembly on August 26 and suspended the constitutional article requiring new elections.

Without the hindrance of an assembly, the security law was enacted and used to arrest a number of leftists and three assembly members: 'Ali Rabi'a, held first for only two weeks; Muhsin Marhun, held for five years; and Muhammad Jabir Sabah, arrested in 1976 for three years. Despite the law's provision for a maximum detention of three years, detainees were incarcerated for five, six, and even seven years. After the law had been in operation for four or five years, the government put it aside and simply detained individuals without going through the court procedure.[21]

Functions and Principal Issues of the National Assembly

Legitimation[22]

The Bahraini constitution, modeled largely on that of Kuwait, also specifies that Bahrain shall have a democratic system of government with sovereignty residing in the people, "the source of all powers," who are also to enjoy the right of election. But this declaration is found in the same article as the designation of the state as a hereditary monarchy (Art. 1). It was clear from the beginning that many in the Al Khalifa saw the National Assembly as a necessary appendage of a modern state but sought to describe it in terms of an extension of *shura*, rather than popular participation in policy-making. Despite the suspension of those constitutional articles dealing with the assembly, the regime maintains that it abides by the constitution.

Formalized Majlis

The concept of *majlis* is less applicable to Bahrain than it is to the other Gulf states. To a large degree, this is determined by the dichotomous nature of Bahrain as a sedentary, peasant society dominated by urbanized tribal elements and is underlined by a Sunni-Shi'i sectarian cleavage. The result has been an adversarial relationship between ruling elite and ruled masses, rather than a partnership between relatively equal tribal and merchant communities. The size and ingrown nature of the ruling family has discouraged outside participation in the political process and reduced the principle of *majlis* to simple petitioning. But the indifference and even intolerance of the ruling family toward reasonable demands for reforms or representation forced would-be reformists into extreme positions and confrontation. Once it became clear that the National Assembly would not function as a formalized *majlis*, it was terminated.

Legislative Role

The assembly had little opportunity to develop its constitutional legislative role. In part, this was because the government apparently viewed the assembly's role in the legislative process as little more than advisory. At the same time, however, the confrontational attitude and tactics of the Left (and possibly also the Islamics) diverted the assembly's attention away from approving draft legislation to polemics. Despite the suspension of the assembly, prominent members of the government maintain that the constitution remains valid and that the Council of Ministers has assumed the legislative function of the assembly. They acknowledge, however, that the cabinet cannot take on the assembly's role in providing checks-and-balances and indicate that the assembly eventually will be reconstituted.[23]

Government Accountability

An impasse over accountability probably was at the heart of the assembly debacle. The regime apparently never contemplated any degree of real accountability, while the politicized Left and the reformist movement had been demanding, vociferously but unsuccessfully, a formal means of accountability for 20 years. Rather than seeking conciliation or a *modus vivendi*, thereby gradually gaining acceptance of the principle of accountability, the opposition insisted on confrontation with the regime and its representatives. The government, suspicious of the opposition's intentions and fearful of threats to internal security, refused to accept any checks on its policies. The resulting head-on collision between the regime and the popular bloc over the security law virtually guaranteed an end to the democratic experiment.

Incipient Populism

To its credit, the Bahraini regime opted for completely free elections. Because of the inherent restraints of honor, a reluctance to criticize individuals publicly, the Left's superior organization in a system that barred political parties, its success at the polls, and its high visibility in an increasingly rancorous assembly, the goals and opinions of the Left received disproportionate attention during the assembly's lifespan. The case could be made that in this manner public opinion was misrepresented or distorted, but it is also true that there is a long history of legitimate grievances against the regime that have never adequately been laid to rest. Continued (if not intensified) Sunni-Shi'i tensions, combined with the economic recession, called for a forum in which differences could be aired peacefully. Indeed, the history of efforts to secure political participation in Bahrain over the last quarter-century shows that Sunnis and Shi'a can overcome sectarian differences and work together effectively, suggesting that a new National Assembly would do more for sectarian harmony than most any other government measure.[24]

Prospects for Reinstitution

Since 1975, the possibility of reinstitution of the assembly has been the focus of considerable private discussion and articles by intellectuals and political activists. In the late 1970s, before the Iranian revolution, there were positive signs that the government was considering action. At an off-the-record meeting with the press, the heir apparent remarked that the government was actively considering reinstituting the assembly. The amir publicly said that a new municipal law should be enacted in harmony with the principle of elections, at a time when municipal councils were no longer elected. Later, the prime minister chided a leading journalist for the superficial mention that the issue received in the press and hinted that if democracy was desired, it had to be discussed fully and the background to democracy in Bahrain explained. Consequently, a series on the history of political participation in the amirate, mentioning that municipal councils had been elected as early as 1925 and that women had voted in 1930, was published in *Akhbar al-Khalij*.

Consideration of a new National Assembly was tempered with plans for safeguards to prevent what the government saw as the excesses of the old one. One suggestion was that the government appoint the assembly members from elected municipal councils. Alternatively, voters could elect a list of 100 candidates, from which the government would choose 30. The possibility of an appointed consultative council was considered as well, particularly because Saudi Arabia appeared to have given its approval to such a body. In those years, it was widely thought that Bahrain was closely following Kuwait's lead and would not act until

Kuwait did. But then the revolution transformed Iran and the government's attitude changed.[25]

Although the supercharged atmosphere of the 1980s further reduced the possibility of a new National Assembly, it did not put an end to discussion. In fact, discussion intensified because of concern over the impact of the Iranian revolution and Iran-Iraq war, the reconstitution of Kuwait's National Assembly, and hints at the establishment of a consultative council in Saudi Arabia. Foreign Minister Shaykh Muhammad ibn Mubarak Al Khalifa declared in 1980 that the return of democracy had been under discussion within the ruling family and government, as well as with Kuwait and Saudi Arabia, and he hoped that the National Assembly would be returned by the end of that year.[26] In retrospect, it is not surprising that nothing happened.

While acknowledging the reconvening of the National Assembly in Kuwait, government apologists stress the considerable differences between Kuwait and Bahrain. Kuwait has had a much longer tradition of a National Assembly, its large non-Kuwaiti Arab population has prompted Kuwaitis to demand political participation, and Kuwait has been able to take a strong stance in the Iran-Iraq war, clearly supporting Iraq. Bahrain, however, was formerly claimed by Iran and, given its numerous Iranian citizens as well as long-standing Arab Sunni-Shi'i differences, must move carefully to avoid inciting either external or internal elements.

The government's position is that it has responded to all the legitimate requirements of its people. According to this view, the average Bahraini first wants education and health care (which the government has provided), a job (and Bahrain presents sufficient opportunities), then land and a house. (If he cannot afford a house, the government can provide housing in 'Isa Town or Hamad Town; otherwise, the housing bank provides loans with nominal interest or the amir may give plots of land directly to petitioners.) The argument is made that Bahrain is able to carry out social programs to a far greater degree than even the socialist countries of Europe because of help from its neighbors, especially Saudi Arabia. The government believes that demands for political participation will not come until later—and at that time the National Assembly will be reformed to meet the citizenry's needs.[27]

The debate is renewed occasionally in the press. After describing the 1985 elections in Kuwait, an editorial in *al-Mawaqif* opined that the democratic approach in Kuwait provided the best means of dealing with events in the Gulf. Democracy was a vital necessity—a filter ridding the air of impurities—and the amir and prime minister were urged to follow Kuwait's example.[28] At the same time, under the headline, "Democracy is Not Contradictory to the State!" *Sada al-Usbu'* reported that the amir told a member of the Kuwaiti National Assembly that democratic life would return to Bahrain, the prime minister was quoted affirming that there was thought of a democratic system, and the heir apparent remarked that the amir's approval of the constitution meant that parliamentary life would not stop, despite temporary adverse circumstances. The author of an accompanying article compared the National Assembly experiment to a feast, to which the Bahraini people were invited 10 years previously. If the meal was not well cooked at that time, then the intervening years were more than sufficient to finish the cooking and to set the tables and invite the people to partake. Democracy was the only means of dissolving the differences between the government and the people.[29]

But these occasional signals produced no discernible movement and no real prospects. Most Bahrainis appear to favor the assembly's return, and government ministers even mention it favorably in conversation. The lack of National Assembly debates, other public forums for discussion of significant issues, and even a vigorous press are blamed for the social and intellectual dormancy, as well as economic and political stagnation. The absence of healthy debate is particularly acute given that the architects of Bahrain's development policy, and most ministers and their undersecretaries have been in office since independence. At the same time, the majority of Bahrainis seem to be resigned to the continuation of the present situation. Attention remains focused on pursuing material opportunities during the receding oil boom, rather than on political participation.

The recent dissolution of the Kuwaiti assembly for the second time also argues against a return to democratic life in Bahrain. The government seems to be most concerned with and still uneasy over the impact of the economic recession and what renewed external pressures might produce in terms of discontent. Wide publicity was given to the pre-emptive discovery of a coup attempt in 1981; a number of arms caches and intrigues have been discovered in the intervening years. Even optimists, who point to those members of the government and ruling family who look favorably on democracy but have not yet found the ideal model to pursue, have resigned themselves to no assembly until external conditions improve and perhaps not before Shaykh Hamad ibn 'Isa succeeds to the throne. That could be several decades away.

4

The Consultative Councils
of the Lower Gulf

Qatar

In contrast to Kuwait and Bahrain, Qatar has emerged as a
distinct political entity only relatively recently. Its predom-
inant ethos is bedouin, not commerce, and its population is
overwhelmingly Sunni Arab tribal, although in recent decades the small commercial community of Doha has been
supplemented by Bahrainis and both Persian and Arab
Shi'a. Nevertheless, the total citizenry may number only
70,000 out of a total population of less than 300,000. The
high degree of homogeneity of its people, common tribal
consciousness, and a favorable ratio of abundant oil income
to tiny population has protected Qatar from the sociopoliti-
cal tensions of Bahrain and even Kuwait.[1] The social homogeneity is reinforced by a common conservative outlook,
since most Qataris are *Muwahhidun* (Wahhabis) and the
socioeconomic change set in train by oil came late to the
amirate.

The leadership of the giant ruling Al Thani family has
been unchallenged since emerging in the mid-nineteenth
century. The present amir, Khalifa ibn Hamad, deposed his
indifferent cousin, Ahmad ibn 'Ali, in February 1972. There
are few decisions made in Qatar except by the amir person-

ally, and Shaykh Khalifa's sound judgment and "workaholic" habits have stood him in good stead with his subjects. The heir apparent, Shaykh Khalifa's son Hamad, will likely reign in similar fashion.[2]

Some popular demand for a representative body appeared as early as the 1950s, and, in response, an Advisory Council was appointed in 1964. The ruler was to serve as president of the council and the deputy ruler as vice president. Its membership of 15 was drawn entirely from the Al Thani and balanced to represent all the branches of the family.[3] The council never met although it provided a precedent for the later creation of a broader council.

Background

A provisional constitution was issued on April 2, 1970 in anticipation of independence. The failure of the Union of Arab Emirates to materialize and Qatar's separate independence required constitutional changes upon Shaykh Khalifa's accession. Consequently, the amended provisional constitution of April 19, 1972 was enacted for a "period of transition"; it still remains in force.[4] Reference to Qatar as a member of the proposed nine-member Union of Arab Emirates (as declared in Arts. 1 and 5 of the original constitution) were eliminated from the amended constitution. The state is described as democratic, Arab, and Islamic, with the *shari'a* as the fundamental source of legislation (Art. 1). Executive power is vested in the amir (Art. 18), judicial power in the courts (issuing judgments in the name of the amir; Art. 19 of the first constitution but not mentioned in the second), and legislative power implicitly in the amir, who is to promulgate laws on the recommendations of the Council of Ministers and the advice of the Advisory Council (Art. 17).

Rulership is declared hereditary within the Al Thani (Art. 21). The original wording, which named Shaykh Khalifa ibn Hamad, the then-deputy ruler, as heir apparent, was changed to a vaguer formula. The description of the duties

of deputy ruler, including serving as prime minister (originally Art. 26), were excised from the amended version and
the office of prime minister entrusted to the amir (Art. 33).
The amir has the sole right to appoint and dismiss the
Council of Ministers (Arts. 28–29).

The constitution also describes the formation and duty
of a consultative council in detail (Arts. 40–64). It has no
explicit legislative function but expresses opinions in the
form of recommendations (Art. 40). At the same time, however, the council is given the power to debate draft laws,
debate general state policies and draft budgets, and put
questions to the Council of Ministers or to individual ministers on matters within their competence (Art. 51). The amir
may dissolve the council, provided a new council is formed
within a month (Art. 61), and dismiss individual members
(Art. 62). The original provisional constitution provided for
the election of a council similar to those of Kuwait and
Bahrain, consisting of 20 elected members and the ministers as ex officio members (Art. 44). Four candidates were to
be elected in each of 10 districts, from which the ruler was
to choose two to represent that district in the council; it also
mandated elections within 30 days of the constitution coming into effect (Art. 45). Elections were never held, and the
amended constitution only refers to elections by direct secret ballot within 60 days of the expiry of the council's term
of office (Art. 46).

The Advisory Council (*Majlis al-Shura*) was formed
soon after the accession of Shaykh Khalifa ibn Hamad as
amir in 1972.[5] Initially, the council consisted of 20 appointed members, plus the cabinet as ex officio members,
but it was expanded to 30 appointed members in 1975.[6]
Technically, there has been only one council since its establishment in 1972, thus circumventing the need to hold elections according to the constitution. Originally convened to
serve for a single year (May 1, 1972 to April 30, 1973), its
life was extended for a further three years (i.e., to April 30,
1975) by an amiri decree immediately before its term was

up. Since then, the council has been extended at regular intervals: until 1978, until 1982, until 1986, and until 1990.

As a consequence, the council members are those appointed in 1972 and 1975. There have been only four new appointments, necessitated by the deaths of members, and, typically, the new members have been close relatives of the deceased. The council elects its own president, vice president, and "office" (consisting of the president, vice president, and two elected supervisors, who act as an executive committee), as well as standing committees on legal and legislative affairs, financial and economic affairs, public services and utilities, domestic and foreign affairs, and cultural and information affairs. There is also a small secretariat.

Composition of Membership

Because Qatar is a small country, the amir can readily choose members who accurately reflect the country's important constituencies. Members are consciously chosen to represent the merchant community (seven members), important tribes (10 members), the educated (six members, five of whom were appointed when the council was expanded), and to make sure that outlying districts are represented (five members).[7] At one point, the government proposed forbidding public servants to hold membership in the Advisory Council, but the council advised against it because Qatar's population is so small and the country needs to utilize fully its few educated people.[8]

The idea that national councils embody a formal version of the *majlis* comes closest to the truth in Qatar. Not accidently, all of Qatar's important constituencies are closely reflected in the Advisory Council's membership, and the members represent their constituencies in the Advisory Council in much the same way they always had done so in the ruler's traditional *majlis*. Undoubtedly the amir seeks the advice or opinion of many of the same people on an informal basis as the government does formally. Because opinions have been voiced already and issues thrashed out privately in the amir's *majlis*, the likelihood of controversy surfacing in the council's deliberations is reduced significantly and consensus is more apt to be obtained. The comparison between *majlis* and council is reinforced by holding the proceedings *in camera* and not reporting the deliberations in the press or showing them on television (as elsewhere in the Gulf) and because vacancies (which occur only upon death) are filled by sons or brothers, thus ensuring continued representation for the constituency.

The personal standing and the representativeness of the council's members are such that any elections quite likely would produce a similar roster of members. As a younger, educated Qatari noted, in any election between himself and an elder, respected Qatari, the elder undoubtedly would win. The continued veneration of age and its associated wisdom is reflected in the choice of the speaker, 'Abd al-'Aziz ibn Khalid al-Ghanim. A council member remarked that al-Ghanim may be an old man but he is like a father, with the implication that the country needs a father figure in such a position.

This situation will not hold forever, of course. Now, when a member dies, he is replaced by a member of his family or tribe. But soon, the present generation of elders or traditional Qataris will be gone and the families and tribes will have to agree on younger individuals, now in their 40s, whose outlooks may not be quite the same. This transformation received an official boost in 1975 when an additional 10 members, most of them younger and educated, were appointed to the council to diffuse the consistent traditionalist domination of the council's vote on nearly every issue.

But even the educated representatives tend to be conservative. One of the most prominent members of the council is the under secretary in the Ministry of Education, 'Abd al-'Aziz 'Abdullah ibn Turki. While he is educated and a competent modernist government official, he is also said to be concerned with inculcating traditional Islamic values in Qatar's schools, in much the same manner as his minister (a member of the Al Thani). Thus, he fits easily into the Advisory Council milieu whereas a more out-and-out modernist, such as former Qatar General Petroleum Company head 'Ali al-Jayda, would not.

Legislative Review

Although the Advisory Council is not a parliament or legislature, draft laws proposed by the cabinet are referred to the council for its recommendations, amendments, and revisions, and then returned to the cabinet (which may or may not accept council's changes). The cabinet then submits them to the amir. The government is not constitutionally bound to respect the opinion of the Advisory Council, but it does so approximately 90 percent of the time. In the other 10 percent of the cases, the government normally tries to justify its decision to the council, which then generally accepts the government version. In addition, draft budgets are also sent to the council for review, and its opinion and all decree laws issued during the council's recesses are referred to the council when it returns in session. The council may either approve the decree or recommend that the cabinet issue a new draft law, but it cannot amend the decree itself (although it can approve the decree on condition that the government issues a new law amending certain provisions).[9]

Although the Advisory Council's legislative powers are severely restricted, it has registered its refusal to accept the government's legislation on more than one occasion. In 1974, a draft law on public housing was deemed unsuitable and a new law drawn up by the cabinet at the council's request. More recently, during the 1984–1985 term, decree laws were issued regarding civil service and military pensions. The laws were automatically referred to the council when it came back into session and vigorously opposed on the ground that the plans were not generous enough for Qatari retirees and too generous for non-Qataris. The decree laws were rejected and sent back to the cabinet for redrafting.

Government Accountability

Although debate on political, economic, and administrative policies is limited to matters referred to the council by the government, the council can initiate discussion on social and cultural affairs. In addition, it has the right to request written or oral statements from members of the cabinet (including the prime minister, i.e., the amir), and individual members have the right to submit written questions to ministers and under secretaries regarding the business of their ministries. The minister's answer may be either written or oral. Alternatively, the minister, if present at the council session, may be questioned directly. Although inquiries are only requests, no minister is said to have refused, although it is conceded that questions would not be put to the amir, the heir apparent (who is also minister of defense), or the amir's second son (who serves as minister of finance and petroleum). In any case, the council does not have the right to put a vote of confidence to the government or any minister.[10]

Obviously, this is a far cry from effective accountability. Nevertheless, the Advisory Council is not entirely a rubber stamp. Its defenders point to those instances when legislation was rejected and to the appearance before the council of under secretaries, ministers, and possibly even the amir's brother. Tribal representatives still have influence and they are not afraid to oppose a policy of the government or amir in the Advisory Council, any less than in the *majlis*. One member cites the close attention that the amir pays to the council's activities, including regular inspection of the minutes. Even with the Advisory Council's limitations, he contends, its existence provides a healthy contribution to a system in which the government's policy-making otherwise would be done totally by the cabinet. He compares Qatar with Bahrain, which does not have even an advisory body since the suspension of the National Assembly.

Legitimation

The explicit inclusion in the constitution of provisions for the Advisory Council and the council's 15 years of activity indicate that it does provide a certain measure of legitimation to the regime. This is underscored by the careful selection of its membership to accurately reflect Qatari society and by the amir's readiness to provide it with an active, albeit advisory, role in scrutinizing legislation. Its symbolic role is strengthened by its capabilities as a forum for discussing issues of the day, such as the impact of the recent recession on Qatari citizens. While its cautiousness in keeping its deliberations secret may satisfy the traditional requirement for consensus in public arenas while serving as an indicator of public opinion, this hinders its potential effectiveness as a perceived institution for political participation. Few younger Qataris appear to have a good idea of the council's activities, know that it actually criticizes the government and influences legislation, or realize that the amir listens closely to the council's advice. Of all the Gulf national councils, only that of Qatar refuses to make its sessions public or allows its proceedings to be published.

United Arab Emirates

The UAE was formed as a federation of the small Trucial States in December 1971, following the failure of negotiations for a larger union of Bahrain and Qatar with the Trucial States. Six states (Abu Dhabi, Dubai, Sharjah, 'Ajman, Umm al-Qaywayn, and al-Fujayra) joined together in the independent UAE in December 1971; they were joined by Ra's al-Khayma in March 1972. Abu Dhabi and, to a lesser extent, Dubai have dominated the UAE as the largest and wealthiest of the seven members. The Abu Dhabi amir, Shaykh Zayid ibn Sultan Al Nahyan, has served as the UAE's only president, while Dubai's ruler, Shaykh Rashid ibn Sa'id Al Maktum, has been the only vice president.[11]

A provisional constitution was promulgated at independence, along with the necessary executive and administrative organs for the new federal state, and was amended in 1972 to reflect Ra's al-Khayma's inclusion in the union.[12] It described the UAE as a federal state (Art. 1) and specified the nature of the relationship between the federal entity and the individual amirates, which retain sovereignty over their own territories and territorial waters (Art. 3).

The federal government is given exclusive jurisdiction over foreign affairs; defense and the federal armed forces; security against external and internal threats; federal officials and judiciary; federal finances, taxes, and public loans; the postal, telephone, telegraph, and wireless services; main roads; air traffic control; education; public health and medical services; the currency; and the census (Art. 120). The constitution also reserved legislative jurisdiction for the federal government in labor relations; real estate; banks and insurance; major legislation in penal, criminal, and civil areas; and the importation of arms and ammunition (Art. 121). The federal nature of the state was guaranteed by leaving all powers to the individual amirates except for those explicitly reserved for the federal government (Arts. 116 and 122). Thus, sovereignty and most existing political, economic, and administrative institutions were left in the hands of the member states.

In general, the most effective federal institutions have been those that did not exist previously on the amirate level. The most important of these is the Supreme Council or the Council of Rulers, representing the supreme authority in the state and consisting of all seven rulers or their deputies (Art. 46). As the highest authority, the council reviews and approves all important matters within the UAE. Its decisions require a high degree of consensus, i.e., the approval on substantive matters of at least five of the seven members, including the two most important amirates, Abu Dhabi and Dubai (Art. 49).

The council is empowered to delegate authority to other institutions. It elects the president and vice president of the state from its members for five-year terms (Arts. 51 and 52). Given the rarity with which the council has met in recent years, the president acts virtually alone. He has the authority to appoint the prime minister, the deputy prime minister, and the other members of the cabinet (Art. 54). As of mid-1987, Shaykh Rashid of Dubai served as prime minister, as well as vice president, even though he was incapacitated by terminal illness.

The 1938 Reform Movement in Dubai

The constitutional movement sweeping the Gulf in the late 1930s provided a precedent for a national council in the UAE. The maritime and trading environments of Kuwait, Bahrain, and Dubai had provided their merchant communities with a relative degree of cosmopolitanism and education, as well as a growing desire for political reform. In addition, the decline of pearling, which had thrown much of the Arab littoral into poverty, deepened their economic concerns and prompted them to test their emerging strength.[13]

Dubai was emerging as the commercial and financial center of the Trucial Coast and was ruled by Sa'id ibn Maktum Al Maktum (r. 1912–1958) in a traditional manner, according to the *shari'a* and single-handedly except for an occasional *majlis* called to provide advice. Sa'id's rule, however, had been challenged periodically by members of his own Al Bu Falasa clan, particularly his cousins (and merchants) from the Rashid section who resided in the Dayra quarter, across Dubai Creek from the ruler. The worsening economic climate, resentment at the relative prosperity of the merchants engaged in smuggling along the Persian coast, and the ruler's enforcement of the British-mandated restrictions on arms traffic and slavery (an important source of pearling labor) produced considerable support for these cousins in their differences with Shaykh Sa'id.[14]

The dissident Al Bu Falasa (who included most of the family) incited mass demonstrations against the ruler in March 1938 and the issue of manumission and action taken against certain gunrunners was raised in Shaykh Sa'id's *majlis*. Although a crisis was averted by British intervention, another dispute between the ruler and his cousins flared up again that summer. A list of demands (including a budget and civil list, municipal reforms, an end to the ruler's monopolies, and fixed allowances for the Al Bu Falasa) was presented, and the dissidents turned Dayra into an armed camp, calling for a representative council like the one established in Kuwait in July, with Shaykh Sa'id as a figurehead.

On October 20, 1938, following the arrival of nearby shaykhs and the British Political Agent from Bahrain, Shaykh Sa'id avoided being deposed by agreeing to the establishment of a consultative *majlis*, composed of 15 members nominated by the leading members of the Dubai community and with the ruler as its head. By the terms of the agreement, revenue accrued to the state and the ruler was to receive an allowance of one-eighth of the total. The *majlis* was to approve all expenditures, with a majority needed to pass decisions. The *majlis* proceeded to carry out reforms in the customs service, set up municipal and merchants' councils, improve security, and establish three schools. Mindful of the merchant constituency, schemes were begun to improve port facilities and the town's roads.

These measures were taken without any contribution from Shaykh Sa'id, who regarded the *majlis* as an illegitimate body usurping his power and rarely attended its meetings. In addition, it seems clear that the Al Bu Falasa leaders of the reform movement acted in their own self-interest as much as a true desire for administrative and political reform. (The charge was made by disgruntled Dubayyans that a single despot had been replaced by a board of despotism.) The attempt in March 1939 to reduce the ruler's income to a fixed sum of Rs.10,000 was the last straw. A few weeks later, Shaykh Sa'id used the occasion of his son's wedding in Dayra to have loyal bedouin seize control of the town. Several members of the *majlis* were attacked and killed; half of the council surrendered, while the other half fled to Sharjah.[15]

The six-month existence of the Dubai *majlis* resulted in the permanent adoption of some changes, such as needed improvements to the harbor and town. A 15-member advisory council (including five members of the old *majlis* but only seven Al Bu Falasa in all) and a merchants' council were instituted in April 1939. Soon afterwards, Shaykh Sa'id's son Rashid assumed much of the responsibility for governing Dubai, although he did not actually succeed his father until 1958. Seemingly sympathetic to many of the reform movement's goals (while politically opposed to its leaders), Rashid was responsible for transforming Dubai into the lower Gulf's premier commercial center and an oasis of prosperity without oil.

Shaykh Rashid's path was not without obstacles, however. Opposition in the 1950s came from the nebulous National Front (*al-Jabha al-Wataniya*). The front, hardly an organization, began as an Arab nationalist club in Dubai in 1953, with about 35 members drawn from young government and bank employees, as well as some members of the established merchant community, particularly those of Sunni Arab tribal background. The front was opposed to the ruler, as the merchants resisted competition from growing numbers of foreign merchants in Dubai and feared that incipient reforms would impair their ability to make money. The younger members, out of a total of an estimated 500 adherents and sympathizers in 1956, placed more emphasis on pan-Arabism and opposition to the British imperialists. An alliance was forged with Shaykh Juma ibn Maktum Al Maktum before he was exiled in 1955 amidst fears that he was preparing a coup against his brother, Dubai ruler Shaykh Sa'id ibn Maktum, and allegedly with the Saudis, who had occupied part of the nearby Buraimi oasis from 1952 to 1955.[16]

The Federal National Council

The origins of the UAE's national council go back to the 1968–1971 negotiations for federation between Bahrain, Qatar, and the seven amirates now composing the UAE. These negotiations foundered for a number of reasons (leading to the separate independence of Bahrain and Qatar), but key among the causes was an inability to agree over the allocation of seats in the proposed Federal Council. The assembly subsequently saw life within the UAE as the Federal National Council (FNC – *al-Majlis al-Watani al-Ittihadi*), which first met in February 1972. The 40 seats are distributed proportionately among the seven amirates, with Abu Dhabi and Dubai each receiving eight, Sharjah and Ra's al-Khayma each receiving six, and four apiece designated for the three remaining amirates. Each ruler chooses the members allocated to his amirate, who serve for two years and may be reappointed. The council elects its own president, two deputies, two rapporteurs, and eight standing committees.[17]

Composition of Membership

The great majority of FNC members are businessmen. Many of the representatives from Dubai, Sharjah, and Ra's al-Khayma come from prominent, urbanized old merchant families, while the other amirate's members tend to be of tribal background who entered commerce on their own.[18] Two members are brothers of federal ministers. The speaker is Hilal Ahmad Luta, from a Dubayyan family of traditional pearl merchants of Indian Liwatiya origin. His predecessor, Tiryam 'Umran Tiryam, was allegedly removed as speaker and FNC member in the early 1980s for being too outspokenly pro-federalization.[19] Most members were educated in the traditional manner, although several of the old members are from the first generation of UAE citizens to receive modern education at the beginning of the oil age. During the 1984–1986 session, the FNC boasted four university graduates, including one from the new UAE University in al-'Ayn.[20]

Legislative Review

By provision of the constitution, all federal legislation, including budgets, is referred to the FNC, which may approve, amend, or reject draft bills (Arts. 89 and 90). The UAE president, with the concurrence of the Council of Rulers, however, may promulgate a bill over the FNC's objections (Art. 110). As such, the council plays a strong advisory role, and is not merely a rubber stamp. Moreover, the government needs to pay close attention to the FNC because the council's members are all fairly important people among the small number of UAE citizens.

The range of the FNC's business is indicated by the following summary at the end of the 1982–1983 sitting: 16 draft federal laws were approved (covering the regulation of insurance companies, the pharmaceutical profession and pharmaceutical establishments, medical practice by nondoctors, charges for health services, and scholarships and educational assistance). Twelve meetings were held in the second half of the session, during which six general issues relating to government policies in the fields of justice, communications, security, information, and encouragement of national contractors were discussed, and an extraordinary session was held on state security policy.[21]

The FNC does not always meekly approve draft laws submitted to it. For example, a number of stormy debates accompanied the article-by-article process of approving the country's penal code, making it the most debated legal document in the history of the UAE. In particular, objections were raised to an article providing for up to 10 years of imprisonment for membership in subversive organizations on the grounds that the provision could jeopardize legitimate democratic activities, discussion on the permanent constitution, and calls for economic reform. A related article proposing stiff penalties for the establishment of organizations without government consent, as well as for membership in any unapproved organization even while outside the country, was roundly attacked as abridging the personal rights and liberties of UAE citizens. Although the articles eventually were passed, they had been amended by the minister of justice, who had been present during the debates.[22]

Government Accountability

The FNC has become more vociferous in recent years, particularly with the UAE's deepening economic problems. In the summer of 1986, the council sent a memorandum to the Supreme Council of Rulers stressing the necessity for certain changes, including the need for economic diversification and an end to duplication of administrative institutions on both the federal and amirate level.

The constitutional provision that the government should be represented in FNC meetings whenever requested has also been taken quite seriously by the council. Members of the FNC complained publicly in 1983 that the constitution had been violated when the minister of education failed to respond to an FNC request for his presence at a meeting to discuss the dismissal of a number of teachers in the midst of a serious shortage of teaching staff. This may have been an aberration, however, for the government was represented during a 1984 meeting when the minister of state for finance and industry answered members' questions on the UAE's financial situation and contributions to the federal budget. This was followed by a reading of the written response of the minister of state for interior affairs on the six-month "stay away" rule for expatriates seeking to change jobs in the UAE. At another meeting in 1985, the minister of state for interior affairs presented and defended a statement on internal security matters during a closed-door session. Afterward, the council called upon the federal government to release the federal budget, appealed to the amirates to honor their assessed contributions to the federal budget, and called for the formation of a committee to prepare a permanent constitution.[23]

Incipient Populism

Debates in the most recent FNC have echoed those of Kuwait's National Assembly, with considerable concern expressed for the vulnerability of poor citizens to the economic recession. Calls were made for the reduction of utility charges, suspension of the law prohibiting ownership of more than one taxi, and government action to increase the number of jobs available to citizens. On at least one occasion, council members spoke up on behalf of expatriate government officials trapped by bureaucratic Catch-22s.[24] Such discussion provides a significant barometer of public opinion, particularly of the lower strata of citizenry who have benefitted the least from the years of plenty, as well as providing a guide for remedial government action.

The National Consultative Council

The direct correlation between *vox populi* and the national councils is even clearer in the case of Abu Dhabi. The existence of a National Consultative Council (NCC – *al-Majlis al-Istishari al-Watani*) for just the amirate of Abu Dhabi illustrates the limited penetration of the federal process in the UAE. Originally composed of 46 appointed members, the NCC was expanded to 50 members in 1983. The NCC does not enjoy the power of legislative review as does the UAE's FNC, although most legislation drafted by the Abu Dhabi Executive Council (the amirate's equivalent of a cabinet) is sent to the NCC.

Its appointees are more closely drawn from the ranks of tribal shaykhs than the FNC (perhaps reflecting Abu Dhabi's more exclusively tribal society), as is its speaker, Shaykh Sultan ibn Surur al-Dhahiri. The size of the various tribes in the Abu Dhabi amirate determines the numbers of

their representatives in the NCC. Because NCC membership is drawn from the tribal establishment, the ruler's appointment of new members to fill vacated seats is more in
the nature of confirming tribally nominated candidates
than freely selecting his own. Some in the NCC hold that
this gives their body more power than the FNC, whose
members serve solely at the pleasure of the seven rulers.[25]

Because its role is less one of government accountability and legislative review (and probably also because of the
nature of its membership), NCC deliberations tend to be
devoted to such populist issues as government assumption
of citizens' debts to banks, multiple taxi ownership, low-
cost housing, water and electricity charges for low-income
citizens, and water shortages.[26]

Future Political Participation

The desired degree of political participation appears to dif-
fer considerably among member amirates. Abu Dhabians
tend to regard traditional means of participation, such as
direct petitioning of the ruler and principal government officials (who are, after all, Al Nahyan shaykhs), as acceptable
in what remains a strongly tribal society. Dubayyans and
Sharjans, on the other hand, relatively more cosmopolitan
and less tribal, may find such traditional expressions
anachronistic or irrelevant. Indeed, even the success of
Dubai's merchant community in acquiring a voice in en-
hancing the pro-commerce attitude of the amirate may not
satisfy younger Dubayyans, whose education and careers
diverge from those of the traditional merchants. Sharjah's
ruler, Shaykh Sultan ibn Muhammad al-Qasimi, has experi-
mented with neighborhood councils to represent the views
and grievances of inhabitants to the ruler directly.[27] In addition, he reportedly has considered permitting the election of
a municipal council and the amirate's FNC members.
On the federal level, the smaller amirates may regard
strengthened popular institutions as a way of abating the
imbalance of power between them and Abu Dhabi.

Representative bodies were a feature of the abortive coup attempt in Sharjah in June 1987. The erstwhile usurper and brother of the ruler, Shaykh 'Abd al-'Aziz ibn Muhammad al-Qasimi, proposed a consultative council as part of his reforms.[28] Soon after regaining control, Shaykh Sultan established a 26-member Executive Council, composed of the heads of government departments and other individuals "selected by the ruler from among citizens known for their ability, experience, and integrity."[29] Among the council's assigned tasks were the drawing up of the amirate's general policy, discussing bills and drafting decrees, considering the annual budget and the development plan, and approving oil agreements.

The future evolution of channels and demands for political participation in the UAE unavoidably will be dependent on the progress of federalization. After a decade-and-a-half of existence, the federal momentum in the UAE is balanced precariously between opposing forces. On the positive side, there is the homogeneity of UAE society, the gradual acceptance of the UAE as a functioning entity, the growing competence of some federal institutions, and the advantages derived from membership in a larger entity. At the same time, however, the UAE experiment is endangered by continuing rivalries among the amirates, the increasing indebtedness of the poorer amirates (and Abu Dhabi's increasing willingness and inability to provide financial support), and the entrenched autonomy of the member states in such areas as sovereignty, defense, oil, and finances.

Above all, the UAE faces a serious crisis of leadership, characterized by a virtual vacuum at the top levels in Abu Dhabi and Dubai and the inability of the governing Council of Rulers to meet except in rare and extraordinary circumstances. Serious consternation exists over this federal state of affairs.

Several combined meetings of the FNC and the cabinet in early 1979 produced a joint memorandum to the Council of Rulers (which had not met formally for more than two years), criticizing the numerous obstacles in the path of federalization. It also called for an expansion of the FNC's base in the context of endorsing democratic principles in the UAE.[30] The memorandum's call for the strengthening of federal institutions, the centralization of revenues, and the full unification of the armed forces, as well as the granting of full legislative powers to the FNC, faced strong opposition from the Council of Rulers, while Shaykh Rashid of Dubai told a Kuwaiti newspaper that "a unitary state means no borders, therefore no rulers. It means elections, it means putting finance, revenue and decision-making in the hands of a central government."[31]

Discussion of the memorandum within the Council of Rulers was accompanied by popular demonstrations for greater unification, although abrupt centralization of the UAE was rejected. Similar demonstrations occurred in following years. This combination of uncertainties regarding succession, the future of the federal process, and strong tensions between the member states does not augur well for the growth and robustness of formal democratic institutions.

Oman

The sultanate form of government in Oman is a radical departure from the imamate, headed by elected *imams* (religious and secular leaders) of the Ibadi sect, which formed Oman's traditional government for nearly a thousand years. The sultans in Muscat survived various attempts in the late nineteenth and early twentieth centuries to reconstruct the imamate chiefly because of British protection. This British influence was also a primary factor in the tacit adoption of primogeniture as the means of succession within the Al Bu Sa'id ruling family. Over the course of the twentieth century, the power of succeeding sultans has increased simultaneously with the diminishing influence of the rest of the ruling family. Since the demise of the imamate and reunification of the country in the 1950s, the political role of the tribes has been minimal, and challenges to the ruler within Muscat nonexistent. A serious rebellion in the southern province of Dhufar, which began as a reaction to the repressive former sultan, was put down in late 1975 after considerable fighting. To a far greater degree than elsewhere in the Gulf, Sultan Qabus clearly stands alone at the apex of authority in Muscat.[32]

Background and Membership

The Sultanate of Oman's State Consultative Council (SCC – al-Majlis al-Istishari lil-Dawla) is the youngest national council in the GCC.[33] The concept of shura (consultation), with its Islamic connotations, was an integral element in the Ibadi imamate but the newer sultanate, based on the Al Bu Sa'id dynasty, has never developed a tradition of consultation, let alone formal representation. Thus, the formation of a small ministerial committee by Sultan Qabus in late 1980 to draw up plans for an assembly was unexpected (and easily kept secret). Following submission of their report, the sultan issued decrees on October 18, 1981 establishing the SCC and appointing its members.[34]

Initially, the council was composed of 43 members but was expanded to 55 in 1983. The original SCC committee is responsible for selecting the members and sending their names to the sultan, who has accepted every nominee for all three SCC sessions. Only the SCC's president is directly chosen by the sultan, so far for two-year terms; the president always holds the rank of minister because he must have direct access to the sultan.

Nineteen members (including the president) belong to the government, comprising the 11 under secretaries of the social service ministries and seven other officials nominated at large (and consisting mostly of "elders").[35] The Chamber of Commerce elects 19 candidates, from which the SCC committee chooses 11 members. Each of the sultanate's seven geographic regions is represented by a varying number of members according to its population size and development needs; the number ranges from seven for the Batina coast to two for the Musandam enclave. Despite the manner of their appointment, these 25 members officially represent all of Oman. The member of the SCC guiding committee from a particular region (or the one most familiar with that region) is responsible for choosing a list of 12 candidates, from which the whole committee selects the region's representatives.[36] During the first session, the 44 members included 24 Ibadis, 13 Sunnis, and 7 Shi'a. Twenty-two had received some modern education, with six having attended university; their median age was 47.[37]

The only permanent members are the 11 under secretaries; even the other seven government representatives can only serve for a maximum of two terms (i.e., four years). The remaining block of 36 members, who are limited to two terms, is rotated so that one-third is replaced every term. The original intention was to provide for a greater range of participation. If a member from the interior, for example, could remain in the council indefinitely, he might be more likely to join "the establishment" than represent his constituents, and younger aspirants would be discouraged from seeking office themselves.

After the first two terms were completed, the need for adjustment was recognized. The under secretaries tended to act as defenders and protectors of the government in general and their ministries in particular. To counteract this, they were granted immunity and encouraged to raise criticisms of all parts of the government – except their own ministries – and indeed were forbidden to participate in issues regarding their own ministries. As a longer term remedy, the SCC committee recommended that the under secretaries be moved around ministries and that newer, more earnest individuals be appointed regularly as under secretaries. At the same time, it was seen that frequent and complete turnover of the other SCC members destroyed continuity and weeded out the few, capable, educated, energetic members, replacing them with less qualified people. It seemed wasteful to disenfranchise members who had developed skills in dealing with a complex government structure, evaluating development projects, and formulating policy recommendations. As a consequence, the sultan privately informed the committee that they could reappoint a particular member for another 2 two-year terms after he had stood down for a term.

Legislative Review

Despite all this elaborate preparation, the SCC has perhaps the most restricted national council mandate in the GCC. In part, this derives from the infrequent, highly formal nature of its meetings. Only three sessions are held each year; each session lasted only three days until 1985, when the period was extended to five days or a week. As originally conceived, all meetings were held *in camera* and the council's competence restricted to economic and social matters. Because the SCC is not in session most of the year, there is little scope for discussion and debate.[38] Consequently, if a member wishes to raise an issue during the 48–49 weeks the SCC is not in session, he must submit a letter to the SCC's Executive Committee (composed of the president and his two deputies as ex officio members, plus another five members elected by the council). This committee may then pass the matter on to the appropriate standing committee, which returns its recommendation to the Executive Committee, which adds its own recommendations and sends it on to the appropriate ministry. The committees have met much more regularly than the SCC as a whole.[39]

SCC recommendations during its first session dealt with the improvement of health services, land affairs, road and highway priorities, the marketing of agricultural products, housing, traditional fishing, encouragement of individual investments, the status of the Jabal al-Akhdar region, and studies prepared by the Board for the Settlement of Commercial Disputes, the Tender Board, and the Electricity Authority. During the following session, recommendations were concerned with changes in the banking sector, incentives for higher education, establishment of boarding schools in remote areas, expansion of post and telephone services, municipal services outside the capital area, agricultural and livestock development, vocational training, the role of the private sector in development efforts, and review of the 1986–1990 development plan and the draft commercial law.[40]

This highly restricted format has been relaxed significantly in the third term (1985–1987), and the first step toward legislative review has been introduced. Draft legislation in the economic and social fields is sent from the cabinet to the SCC for consideration in the appropriate committee, then discussed during the regular terms and recommendations voted on for dispatch to the sultan. The sultan chooses whether to accept these recommendations or not (he is said to have accepted every one to date), and then passes them back to the cabinet for its comments and implementation. In matters concerning the development plan, recommendations are sent by the sultan to the Development Council to comment on their feasibility and then to the appropriate ministry for implementation. Theoretically, if the recommended improvement cannot be carried out at the time, perhaps for financial reasons, then the recommendation is incorporated into the five-year plan.[41] It is worth noting that this new legislative role does not include defense, foreign affairs, or apparently even oil, nor does it include the power of veto. The third-term SCC has reviewed the state's draft budget.

Incipient Populism

Another recent development has been the end to secrecy by reporting and televising the formal sessions. This, in its modest way, appears to have laid some groundwork for an SCC role as government watchdog. Ministers are required to appear before the SCC when a matter concerning their ministry is discussed, and they must reply on the spot to valid questions put by any member of the SCC. Of course, only the heads of the social service ministries are account-able, and neither they nor the government can be put to a vote of confidence. Even more than elsewhere in the Gulf, the ultimate authority of the ruler is unquestioned.

Government Accountability

The mixing of government and non-government members raises the question of conflict of interest, not only in regard to the under secretaries but also to the president. Because the president is head of the SCC for only two years, he has no real stake in the consultative process. Because he is a minister, both by virtue of his personal rank and by past and future positions, he is more a member of the govern-ment than a watchdog.[42] Another area of conflict of interest arises from the tendency of some ministers to use their official positions to advance their personal business. How can a president support measures of personal accountabili-ty among officials when it may involve him and his past and future colleagues, it is asked. The representational compre-hensiveness of the SCC can be questioned as well, given the secretive nature of the members' selection.

Legitimation

It is difficult to determine whether the formation and ac-tivities of the SCC have contributed to the legitimacy of the state. In a sense, the SCC has carved out a modest niche through the petitions submitted to it by individuals and groups of citizens, who may also question members from their region. The exclusion of such areas of government activity as defense, foreign affairs, and oil from the council's competence is defended by the government on the grounds that the SCC is too new to entrust it with such sensitive matters. Presumably, the SCC's purview may be increased in future years. Beneath it all runs the knowledge that Oman, far more than its GCC neighbors, is a one-man mon-archy whose authority is virtually unchallenged by the ruling family, other notable tribal or merchant families, or even the cabinet. One area in which the council could conceivably provide a benefit is discussion over the question of succession, but this is the most sensitive area of all. It is to the sultan's credit that he established the SCC and has pushed for its acceptance within the Omani political system, often against the reluctance of other family members and ministers.

5

Changing Expectations and the Role of National Councils

There is a long background to formally constituted national councils in the Gulf. Although the reform movements of 1938 in Kuwait, Bahrain, and Dubai were unsuccessful in securing power-sharing, the underlying factors provoking their development prompted later efforts at reform. Complaints about the Al Sabah-dominated government emerged in Kuwait in the mid-1950s. The creation of the Higher Executive Committee in Bahrain in 1954 and the unsatisfactory denouement of that movement in 1956 has already been examined in detail. Similarly, a nationalist movement was reported in Dubai in 1955.[1] These earlier movements and other means of political expression have provided the impetus for the creation of national councils since the 1960s. Although the power of the councils has been relatively marginal, their impact has been significant, and their place in the changing political structure of the GCC states should not be underestimated.

The Role of Strikes and Demonstrations

To a certain extent, reform activities were tied to economic grievances, particularly among pearl-divers at the beginning and in the oil sector in later years. Kuwait experienced strikes among the oil and transportation workers in 1948 over the issue of discrimination compared to foreign workers, and in December 1953 by 900 Indian and Pakistani oil workers.[2] The tense political atmosphere in Bahrain of May 1955 included a short strike by 200 oil workers in 'Awali.[3]

In Saudi Arabia, some 70 percent of the 1,400 Arab employees of ARAMCO, as well as 60 percent of those at the U.S. air base at Dhahran, went on strike in October 1953 over the arrest of six leaders of an unapproved workers' committee. The strike, which lasted over a month, involved both political issues and economic grievances, particularly in the demand for benefits similar to those received by American employees, and some indication of leftist influence was claimed. The only violent incident involved the stoning of a bus filled with Saudi troops from the Dhahran air base. All the leaders appeared to be Saudi nationals (with one apparently educated in the United States by ARAMCO), except for one Iraqi. After a brief imprisonment, the Saudis were sent back to their villages and the Iraqi deported.[4] The following year, a rash of antigovernment pamphlets sparked the arrest of approximately 30 people in Jidda, Riyadh, and Dhahran.[5]

About 20 percent of ARAMCO employees struck again in June 1956 for several days, and several petitions, including demands for an elected workers' committee and for the closure of the U.S. air base at Dhahran, were presented to King Sa'ud. Stones were thrown at the king's car when he visited Dhahran. Riots during the same period at a cinema in nearby Ra's Tanura resulted in the flogging to death of four men and the imprisonment and torture of another 60. The government reacted strongly to the disturbances by publishing a royal decree on June 22, which declared strikes illegal and punishable by one–three years imprisonment.[6]

A strike broke out at the Qatar Petroleum Company's Dukkan operations in August 1955 over the Qatari drivers' objections to two Indian transport clerks. When the strikers seized some company cars used by the European staff, a police detachment led by a British inspector attempted to recover them. A melee ensued, several policemen were injured, and the inspector was struck unconscious. When news of the strike spread to Umm Sa'id, the workers struck there as well, forcing the British employees out of their offices and shutting down the power plant. The ruler's representative was able to convince the strikers to return to work on the following day, and a rumored strike among government employees in Doha failed to materialize. As an indication of the manner in which the ruler's attention to governing was regarded, the strikers' demands were addressed to Shaykh Khalifa ibn Hamad, the deputy ruler (now the amir), who declined, however, to challenge the ruler. A list of 11 demands, mostly economic, was presented to the government, and the ruler was finally able to reconcile the workers and the oil company.[7]

Labor unrest and economic grievances even boiled over in the Sultanate of Oman barely a year after the July 1970 palace coup d'etat that brought Sultan Qabus to power. Matrah, the twin city of the capital at Muscat, was the scene of strikes and demonstrations in September 1971. Although primarily prompted by growing inflation and Omani resentment of the better wages and housing offered to expatriates, the demonstrations were said also to reflect dissatisfaction with the new regime's emphasis on the rebellion in the far-off province of Dhufar and defense expenditures, as well as corruption in high places.[8]

The occurrence of such strikes and agitation have political importance, as they suggest that nontraditional political methods may be employed to protest economic grievances. Strikes among Gulf nationals have become rare since the onset of the oil boom in each country for at least two reasons. First, the economic impetus behind such actions has been undercut by the institution of social welfare societies that have guaranteed the provision of at least basic needs for all nationals. Second, and more important politically, security apparatuses have been vastly improved. Security forces are in a position to know about possible agitation at an advanced stage, and they have the ability to move

quickly and forcefully to nip strikes and other political activities in the bud. Most nationals appear to have no desire
to engage in antiregime activities. Of those who may be so
inclined, subdued discussion among associates or veiled
comments in print form a more prudent course of action.

Moves Toward a Consultative
Council in Saudi Arabia

Although Saudi Arabia has never established a national
council, it has indicated its intention to do so on several
occasions. A precedent existed after 'Abd al-'Aziz Al Sa'ud
conquered the Hijaz in 1924, which had a relatively sophisticated population and government machinery compared to
the Najd. A Consultative Council (al-Majlis al-Ahli) was introduced for Mecca in January 1925, with representatives
of the religious leadership ('ulama'), notables (a'yan), and
merchants — each electing delegates to the 15-member council. It was replaced six months later by a broader council
with two members representing the 'ulama', one representing the merchants, and 12 each representing a different
quarter of the city; another three members were appointed
by the king. Similar councils were announced for the Hijazi
cities of al-Madina, Jidda, al-Ta'if, and Yanbu', and these
councils together with key tribal shaykhs were to elect the
members of a General Consultative Council.

These plans were superseded by the actions of the new
viceroy, Amir (later King) Faysal ibn 'Abd al-'Aziz. A Constituent Assembly, composed of eight elected and five appointed members, was charged with writing a constitution
for the Hijaz, and the resultant " Basic Instructions for the
Hijaz" (al-Ta'limat al-Asasiya lil-Mamlaka al-Hijaziya) was
published on September 3, 1926. This constitutional document provided for the establishment of a Consultative
Council (Majlis al-Shura) for the Hijaz and a number of city
and village councils.

After further amendment of the Basic Instructions, the

Consultative Council was formed in July 1927, with four members chosen in consultation with prominent members of the community, another four appointed by the government (including a stipulated two Najdis), and the viceroy as chairman. Its mandate included reviewing budgetary questions, new projects, and other economic matters and the enactment of laws and statutes. Further changes a year later eliminated the stipulations on consulting community members for some appointments and the necessity of including the Najdis. Its size was increased to 20 members in 1952 and to 25 in 1955. The Consultative Council was joined by a Council of Deputies, essentially a mini-cabinet for the Hijaz, in 1931. The two Hijazi councils continued to administer the affairs of that region until the formation of a kingdom-wide Council of Ministers in October 1953. Although this action made the Council of Deputies superfluous, the Consultative Council continued to meet thrice-weekly into the 1970s.[9]

In the last several decades, the formation of a consultative council has been broached a number of times but never carried into fruition. The proposed but never implemented Organic Law of 1960, an attempt to create a formal constitution for the kingdom, included provisions for a council. This National Council (*al-Majlis al-Watani*) was to consist of 120 members, with 40 to be appointed and 80 indirectly elected through nomination by provincial councils and approved by a committee of 10 appointed by the king.[10] King Faysal announced a resurrection of the old Consultative Council as part of his reform package announced in November 1962 (shortly after the revolution in Yemen).[11] There were indications that the idea was being considered prior to the assassination of King Faysal in March 1975, and a policy statement following the accession of Khalid ibn 'Abd al-'Aziz as king declared that a council, to be composed of about 70 members drawn from professional and official ranks, would be established in two-months time.[12] The issue was raised again in the aftermath of the occupation of Mecca's Great Mosque in January 1980, and a council was promised within two months. The proposed council came within a framework of constitutional reform, which also contemplated a constitution of 200 articles based on the Quran and Sunna (the customs of the Prophet Muhammad).[13]

Finally, King Fahd ibn 'Abd al-'Aziz announced in a 1984 interview that he intended to create the Consultative Council as well as provide a written constitution. A committee headed by Amir Nayif ibn 'Abd al-'Aziz, the interior minister, had presented its recommendations in early 1984, but the decision had been delayed by the opposition of some of the Al Sa'ud and religious interests. But the king stated that the council was to be set up in another "three or four months," initially with an appointed membership. The plan envisaged indirect elections after several years for about half the members through provincial assemblies, and later direct elections for some or all of the membership. Further hints emerged a few months later that the council was on its way, that its members would be chosen from 14 elected regional councils, and that its functions would include approving the budget, discussing laws, and questioning government officials.[14] This was followed by the construction of the King's Office, Council of Ministers, and Assembly Complex in Riyadh. King Fahd, on the eve of his 1987 visit to London, once again affirmed that the assembly would be established soon.[15]

Needless to say, the Consultative Council has yet to appear. In part, the failure to carry through on repeated promises may have been prompted by a reluctance to experiment during trying external circumstances, specifically the Iran-Iraq war. At the same time, there seems to have been considerable concern that an elected assembly (and perhaps even an appointed council) might be dominated by Islamics and made unworkable. There was little concern that an opposition bloc of secular ideologues would appear, as in Kuwait or as feared in the past. But deeper, however, was the underlying fear that public debate would accentuate regional divisions; in this view, there still is no true Saudi, only Najdis, Hijazis, and 'Asiris tied together by the Al Sa'ud. Observers also noted the strength of tribalism and the inability of people even within a region or village to get along, as well as the danger of public criticism of individuals in a society in which such criticism is equated with an attack on one's honor.[16]

The Functions of National Councils

National councils are necessary, functional institutions in the Gulf states for a number of reasons. First, societies and the political and governmental structure have become more complex. The distance between the ruler and the ruled has grown to a greater degree than ever before. There are more constituencies to satisfy, including minorities and the emerging middle class. Second, expectations have changed. This includes expanded conceptions of the proper role of a modern government and altered opinions on the nature of the relationship between ruling families and the citizenry. Changing expectations in the context of the 1980s presages a more independent role for the national councils from control or manipulation by ruling families. Third, while traditional aspects of Gulf societies and politics remain strong, subtle but intensifying modifications in the political structure require the reformulation of the bases of legitimacy. National mythologies may serve to reinforce the position of ruling families, but changing expectations require new formulas. Fourth, national councils represent one aspect of an emerging and necessary process of institutionalization, with its own dynamic and requirements.

As can be seen from the foregoing discussion, the national councils of the Gulf are not entirely rubber-stamp bodies, completely dominated and controlled by the head of state or a small elite group, whether the ruling family or a party organization (as exists elsewhere in the Middle East). Instead, they fulfill real and necessary functions, even if their power and responsibility fall far short of similar bodies in Western democracies. The functions they provide can be summarized as follows:

1. *The Legitimation of the Regime as a "Democracy."*

The Gulf states require new or supplementary manifestations of their legitimacy in the face of rapid, drastic changes. They are no longer purely tribal societies in which tribal elders and notables exercise total authority over uneducated masses. But the actions of the ruling families in Kuwait and Bahrain leave their commitment to constitutionalism open to question. Constitutional sovereignty perhaps is postponable at present, but there is a longer-term question of the viability of monarchies in these developing states. Currently, the political systems of the GCC constitute a transitional stage between traditional authority (with the ruling families' right to rule based on their social standing in a tribal milieu, their long legacy of leadership, and their record of protection of the community and maintenance of law and order), and acquired authority (based on merit and popular support, with leaders serving as the chosen agents of the people in whom sovereignty resides).

2. *A Formalized Majlis.* Traditionally, the *majlis* provided a sounding board whereby the ruler could assess public opinion, receive informal (and nonbinding) advice, and sound out prominent members of the community on ideas and potential policies. In the oil era, the utility of the *majlis* has often been reduced to a ceremonial function of paying one's respects to the ruler or governor, petitioning him for a favor or redress of a grievance, or receiving foreign visitors. Even where the informal *majlis* is maintained as a casual conclave among friends and associates, its usefulness has been eroded by the growing size and complexity of Gulf societies, with their increasing demands upon the individual's time and the decline of traditional social courtesies (such as daily calls upon family elders and community notables).[17]

The national council, then, can be seen as an attempt to preserve the traditional function of the *majlis*, by providing leading representatives of the community with a public forum for discussing important issues and providing the ruler (and the government) with advice and recommendations. This is illustrated most clearly in Qatar's Advisory Council and Abu Dhabi's National Consultative Council. The more political change advances, however, the less relevant this function is likely to become.

3. *The Legislative Role.* In every country, the legislative work carried out by the national council has been limited to legislative review, rather than the initiation of major legislation. The extent of review has varied widely. In Kuwait, near-absolute review has been mandated both by the constitution and by the expectations engendered by history and recent experience. On the other hand, review in the consultative councils is more of a privilege extended by the ruler, or a tool to give a public impression of broader participation in the policy-making process, than a right. All the national assemblies and consultative councils have exercised the right to question members of government, although the prime ministers and portfolio-carrying members of ruling families have been sacrosanct everywhere except Kuwait. The principle of a vote of no-confidence has been an issue only in Kuwait, although never formally invoked. There have been at least two isolated instances of a ruler's veto or decree being overridden: the decision to ban all alcohol in Kuwait, including within embassies, and the rejection of a pension decree in Qatar.

4. *Government Accountability.* The creation of complex, unfamiliar, and often inefficient bureaucracies has prompted national councils to question, criticize, and force governments to execute corrections or changes in general policies and the specific actions of government agencies. Kuwait alone has seen an actual carry-through in its holding the heads of agencies, i.e., cabinet members, responsible for their own actions as well as those of their agencies. In the last assembly, this principle was even on the verge of extension to members of the ruling family, which gave added impetus to the idea that the ruling families should not hold cabinet positions.

More indirectly, the deliberations and decisions of national councils can provide an informal referendum on the government as a whole. This generally goes no further than the cautious expression of comments regarding the quality of life. But the tenor of assemblies in Kuwait and Bahrain, particularly in the vocal opposition provided by leftist members, has served to highlight divisions over the right of the ruling families and their allies to dominate politics and the economy. This again was a large part of the reason that prompted the last dissolution of the Kuwaiti National Assembly.

5. *Incipient Populism*. National councils provide a convenient safety valve for the expression of opinion and grievances. This function is reinforced by their members' role in receiving constituents' requests for assistance and petitions that are introduced in the body or its committees. From another angle, it has become acceptable, even *de rigeuer*, to criticize aspects of government policy as a way of gaining public attention or support. In the case of Kuwait's elected body, nearly all elected members have demonstrated a proclivity for playing to the grandstand. This includes not only the demonstrable opposition but the tribalists as well. In literal terms, their grandstand may be an audience physically present in the assembly chamber of up to a thousand, as well as extensive press coverage and electoral campaigns. Obviously, such criticism enhances the prospects of reelection.

The role of safety valve undoubtedly is as positive as governments perceive it. But there is also a negative aspect to a populist appeal. It may promote confrontation rather than compromise. These are societies that put considerable emphasis on honor and public courtesies. Objective criticism of public figures all too often is perceived as a personal attack. In addition, national councils are more than just a safety valve, but a formal substitute for traditional participation. They directly serve the interests of the state because they serve as forums for the expression of views desired by the state, and the state is able to control the expression of views in the context of assemblies easily.

Generally, however, speaking out in the name of the people is done with caution and often is done with ulterior motives. The speaker not only seeks credibility with a popular constituency but often with the government as well. As a consequence, many members will praise the government for all it has provided and only then ask for a specific improvement, such as a well or school, or inquire why a promised project has been delayed.

6. *The Legitimation of Political Participation by Minority or Non-Elite Groups.* Traditionally power has been shared by ruling families, the shaykhs of important allied tribes, and prominent merchants. Other groups of lesser standing were excluded from a say in policy-making. More recently, however, they have participated fully in national councils, either through the election of representatives from the group or through the deliberate allocation of seats for them by the ruler. Groups that have benefited in this manner include the bedouin; the Shi'a; the Liwatiya and Baluch in Oman and, to a lesser extent, the UAE; and the educated, the technocrats, or the emerging middle class. The continued suspension of the national assemblies in Bahrain and Kuwait is likely to add to sectarian tensions, already aroused by the Iranian revolution and the war, and specifically to an increased Shi'i perception of beleaguerment in an intolerant Sunni system.

The GCC States and Democratic Institutions

Given the existing political systems and the weight of history and tradition in favor of resistance to change by tribal regimes, can formal national councils serve as legitimate forums for criticism? More fundamentally, can they serve as nuclei or catalysts for pluralism and the dispersion of political power? In reviewing the failure to institute electoral bodies in Bahrain and Qatar, Emile Nakhleh has noted the argument that "participatory government and continued authoritarian family rule are by definition contradictory. Sharing in government requires both rights and responsibilities as well as a sincere commitment to the spirit of compromise."[18] He goes on to note that "for democracy to function effectively at least three basic conditions must be fulfilled: the relationship between the government and the governed must be clearly defined; democracy must be recognised as a right that belongs to the people, rather than being a gift from the ruler; and the process must become institutionalised and not subject to the whim of any one ruler on any one ruling family."[19]

Clearly, the governments of the GCC states are not democratic in the sense that West European and the U.S. governments are. Leadership is strictly hereditary, ultimate control of the state is restricted to ruling families, and as of 1987 only three states had national councils—all of whose members were appointed by their respective rulers. It would be a mistake, however, to regard these states as autocratic, repressive, or anachronistic. Rather than being alien creation of colonial overlords and far from being unresponsive to the needs of their people, these regimes are apparently regarded as legitimate by nearly all their citizens. Instead of being relics from the past, all six governments have made drastic adaptations to changing circumstances and expectations. As such, they represent transitional stages in the path of political evolution from traditional to modern societies.

At the same time, the more evolving circumstances require even more radical political transformation, the less the traditional aspects and claims to legitimacy of these regimes will satisfy the demands of their citizens. This is a principal reason why national councils have been created in all but one GCC state and why Kuwait established and then reestablished an elected parliament. Such key democratic institutions as national councils are likely to be increasingly necessary as time goes on, particularly as growing populations and faster-paced lifestyles result in less personal contact between citizens, governments become more complex, access to rulers and ruling families decreases, and informal participation through traditional means, such as the *majlis*, or modern means, such as policy-influencing positions within the bureaucracy, loses relevance or possibility.

The Gulf regimes appear to be cognizant of this necessity, even as they regard it nervously and ambiguously. Amir Jabir of Kuwait, in announcing dissolution of the National Assembly, declared that

> real democracy stems from the principles of *shura*. It is a dialogue with an aim, wise cooperation, understanding, and decision. Democracy is self-denial and correction. In our opinion, . . . Kuwait should exist, first of all, and we are all at its service, protecting it with our bodies and souls. . . . I have seen the picture of democracy shaking, and its practice slipping away, taking with it social and moral norms, and the cohesiveness inherent in the Kuwaiti society disintegrate with it, responsibility has come into disarray and has been wiped out, and the citizens do not know any more who is responsible for the events that are taking place.[20]

It is difficult to predict when changes will occur, or the precise path they will take. The continued suspension of national assemblies and the reluctance to take the step from consultative council to national assembly (or even to create a consultative council) makes taking the step toward true democratic institutions even more difficult. There is a tendency of ruling families in the Gulf to dismiss the importance of political participation in national councils, preferring instead to rely on traditional methods, but this attitude is quickly becoming both outdated and dangerous. As Amir Talal ibn 'Abd al-'Aziz Al Sa'ud remarked in 1986, the Arab world cannot advance "one step" in the absence of democratic freedoms, because progress and prosperity come through democratic life. What is to be feared is that the GCC could become "just another Arab League" if "Gulf citizens are not involved in council meetings, deliberations and resolutions."[21]

Notes

Chapter 1

1. One Kuwaiti has proposed SNAK as a Kuwaiti equivalent to the American WASP: Sunni, Najdi, Arab Kuwaiti. Interview in Kuwait.

2. For overviews of legal development, see Herbert J. Liebesny, "Administration and Legal Development in Arabia: The Persian Gulf Principalities," *Middle East Journal* 10, no. 1 (1956), 33–42; and Nicholas B. Angell, "Impact of the GCC on the Developing Legal Systems of the Gulf Countries," in John A. Sandwick, ed., *The Gulf Cooperation Council: Moderation and Stability in an Interdependent World* (Boulder, Colo.: Westview Press; Washington, D.C.: American-Arab Affairs Council, 1987), 107–144.

3. J. E. Peterson, "Legitimacy and Political Change in Yemen and Oman," *Orbis* 27, no. 4 (Winter 1984), 979.

4. S. N. Eisenstadt draws a clear distinction between "traditional" and "traditionalist." Traditionalism "denotes an ideological mode and stance oriented against the new symbols; it espouses certain parts of the older tradition as the only legitimate symbols of the traditional order and upholds them against 'new' trends. Through opposing these trends, the 'traditionalist' attitudes tend toward formalization on both the symbolic and organizational levels." "Post-Traditional Societies and the Continuity and Reconstruction of Tradition," *Daedalus* 102, no. 1 (1973), 22.

5. Fuad I. Khuri describes this process in *Tribe and State in Bahrain: The Transformation of Social and Political Authority in*

an Arab State (Chicago: University of Chicago Press, 1980), 218–219.

6. Interview with Saudi Interior Minister Amir Nayif ibn 'Abd al-'Aziz for *al-'Arab* (Paris), May 1, 1987, summarized by the Saudi Press Agency (Riyadh), April 30, 1987 (Foreign Broadcast Information Service [FBIS], Middle East and Africa, May 6, 1987).

7. Abdullah Yusuf Ali, *The Holy Qur-an: Text, Translation and Commentary* (New York: Hafner Publishing, 1946), 1317.

8. Ibid., 165. The third form of the verb derived from the root "sh-w-r," i.e., *shāwara*, used in this verse implies a reciprocity in seeking counsel or taking advice, akin to the change of meaning from the first form of "k-t-b," "to write," to the third form, "to correspond with."

9. Text of July 3, 1986 address to the nation published in *al-Watan*, July 4, 1986 (FBIS, July 7, 1986).

10. W. Montgomery Watt, *Islamic Political Thought* (Edinburgh: Edinburgh University Press, 1968; paperback edition, 1980), 35–36.

11. Majid Khadduri, *Political Trends in the Arab World: The Role of Ideas and Ideals in Politics* (Baltimore, Md.: Johns Hopkins University Press, 1970; paperback edition, 1972), 30. See also Albert Hourani, *Arabic Thought in the Liberal Age, 1798–1939* (London: Oxford University Press, for the Royal Institute of International Affairs, 1962).

12. The Ottoman parliament was known as *Meclis-i Meb'usan* (council of delegates), and Arab states have relied on *Majlis al-Umma* (National Assembly), *Majlis al-Nawwab* (Council of Deputies), and *Majlis al-Sha'b* (People's Congress). Within the GCC states, only Qatar uses *Majlis al-Shura*. Kuwait's assembly was known as *Majlis al-Umma*, that of Bahrain as *al-Majlis al-Watani* (National Assembly), and that of the United Arab Emirates as *al-Majlis al-Watani al-Ittihadi* (Federal National Council). Although the discussion of a national council in Saudi Arabia generally has used the term *majlis al-shura*, there is no certainty that the title would be employed if such a body were actually constituted. Oman apparently rejected the use of *shura* to avoid any connotation that the state was bound constitutionally to seek consultation from its assembly and accept its decisions. Instead, it adopted the term *istishari*, derived from the same root as *shura* but connoting "advisory" rather than "consultative" and akin to the title for adviser (*mustashar*). Known in English as the State

Consultative Council, *al-Majlis al-Istishari lil-Dawla* may be translated more literally as "the advisory council for the state." Abu Dhabi's *al-Majlis al-Istishari al-Watani* (National Consultative Council) uses the same term. Note may be made of the choice of the construction, *"lil-dawla"* (i.e., a somewhat ambiguous body that provides advice for the state), rather than, for example, *"majlis al-dawla"* or *"al-majlis al-dawli"* (i.e., an integral organ of the state).

13. James A. Bill and Carl Leiden, *Politics in the Middle East*, 2nd ed. (Boston: Little, Brown, 1984), 28.

14. Ibid.

15. This generalization should not obscure the existence of minorities, such as stateless bedouin, Shi'a (especially in Saudi Arabia and Bahrain), or the Baluch in Oman, who in some respects may form an underclass.

16. Rosemarie Said Zahlan notes the early interrelationship between events in the Arab world and the Gulf states in "The Gulf States and the Palestine Problem, 1936–48," *Arab Studies Quarterly* 3, no. 1 (Winter 1981), 1–21. See also Saeed Khalil Hashim, "The Influence of Iraq on the Nationalist Movements of Kuwait and Bahrain, 1920–1961" (unpublished Ph.D. thesis, University of Exeter, March 1984).

17. Referring to Kuwait, Tawfic E. Farah notes that "the members of a *diwaniya* form a society which operates for their collective benefit. Here, appointments are decided, contracts settled, introductions made, jobs awarded – always in subtly understood ways. Thus, the *diwaniya*'s importance far exceeds its purely social aspect as a staid gentlemen's club." "Inculcating Supportive Attitudes in an Emerging State: The Case of Kuwait," *Journal of South Asian and Middle Eastern Studies* 2, no. 4 (Summer 1979), 61. "Kuwaitis do want to express their thoughts about political matters. They do that at their *diwaniya*s. The ruling elite pay close attention to the mood in the *diwaniya*. Hence, the government has daily public opinion polls." Ibid., 67.

18. The paper was banned for a few days in June 1987 when Shaykh 'Abd al-'Aziz ibn Muhammad al-Qasimi unsuccessfully attempted to overthrow his brother Shaykh Sultan as ruler of Sharjah.

19. Khuri, *Tribe and State in Bahrain*, 218–219.

20. In this connection, it is worth nothing with some puzzlement that the only public records of assembly debates and activi-

ties have been in Kuwait and the UAE. The advantages of providing publicity to the existence and functioning of these bodies would seem to outweigh by far any potential drawbacks of adverse criticism of the government or its representatives.

Chapter 2

1. On the political background to modern Kuwait, see 'Abd al-'Aziz al-Rashid, *Tarikh al-Kuwayt*, ed. and notes by Ya'qub 'Abd al-'Aziz al-Rashid; rev. ed. (Beirut: Manshurat Dar Maktabat al-Haya, 1978); Harold R. P. Dickson, *Kuwait and Her Neighbours* (London: George Allen & Unwin, 1956); Ahmad Mustafa Abu Hakima, *History of Eastern Arabia, 1750–1800: The Rise and Development of Bahrain and Kuwait* (Beirut: Khayats, 1965); idem, *The Modern History of Kuwait, 1750–1965* (London: Luzac, 1983); and Naseer H. Aruri, "Kuwait: A Political Study," *Muslim World* 60, no. 4 (October 1970), 321–343.

2. Ahmed Abdullah Saad Baz, "Political Elite and Political Development in Kuwait" (unpublished Ph.D. dissertation, The George Washington University, 1981), 113–118; Aruri, "Kuwait," 333; and India Office Library and Records (IOLR, London), L/P&S/18/B395, "Koweit, 1908–1928," J. G. Laithwaite, October 1, 1928.

3. IOLR, L/P&S/12/3719, "Persian Gulf Annual Administration Reports 1926–1938"; Baz, "Political Elite," 117–118; and Jill Crystal, "Patterns of State-Building in the Arabian Gulf: Kuwait and Qatar" (unpublished Ph.D. dissertation, Harvard University, 1986), 123–127, who draws extensively on Najat 'Abd al-Qadir al-Jasim, *Baladiyat al-Kuwayt fi khamsin 'am* (Kuwait: Kuwait Municipality, 1980).

4. The following section is drawn from records in the IOLR, including L/P&S/12/3720A, "Persian Gulf Annual Administration Reports, 1939–1945"; L/P&S/12/3894A, "Koweit, Disturbances, 1938; Koweit Council"; R/15/5/205, "Kuwait Situation: Shaikh Ahmad, Council and Reforms (1938)"; R/15/5/206, "Kuwait Situation: Constitution and Council (1938–1949)"; as well as Khalid Sulayman al-'Adsani, *Nusf 'am lil-hukm al-niyabi fi al-Kuwayt* (n.p., 1366/1947); Zahra Freeth and Victor Winstone, *Kuwait: Prospect and Reality* (London: George Allen & Unwin; New York: Crane, Russak, 1972), 118–121; Baz, "Political Elite," 118–130;

Muhammad al-Rumayhi, "Harakat 1938 al-islahi fi al-Kuwayt wa-al-Bahrayn wa-Dubayy," *Majallat Dirasat al-Khalij wa-al-Jazira al-'Arabiya* 1, no. 4 (October 1975), 29–68; Jacqueline S. Ismael, *Kuwait: Social Change in Historical Perspective* (Syracuse: Syracuse University Press, 1982), 71–77; Crystal, "Patterns of State-Building," 127–134; and Saeed Khalil Hashim, "The Influence of Iraq on the Nationalist Movements of Kuwait and Bahrain, 1920–1961" (unpublished Ph.D. thesis, University of Exeter, March 1984).

5. The choice of 'Abdullah may have been a disguised attempt to make him regent. Shaykh Ahmad displayed little interest in administration and used his Persian *wazir* (Mulla 'Abdullah Salih) and the latter's son to handle affairs and represent him in minor matters. Meanwhile, 'Abdullah already served as town administrator, judge, head of police, director of education, and director of land customs.

6. The council members were al-Haji Muhammad al-Thunayan al-Ghanim, 'Abdullah al-Hamad al-Saqr, Shaykh Yusuf ibn 'Isa, al-Sayyid 'Ali al-Sayyid Sulayman, Mish'an al-Khudayr al-Khalid, 'Abd al-Latif Muhammad al-Thunayan, Sulayman Khalid al-'Adsani, Yusuf Marzuq al-Marzuq, Salih al-'Uthman al-Rashid, Yusuf al-Salih al-Humaydi, Muhammad al-Da'ud al-Marzuq, Sultan Ibrahim al-Kulayb, Mashari Hasan al-Badr, and Khalid al-'Abd al-Latif al-Hamad. The "Law Governing the Powers of the Kuwait Administrative Council" (1) named the people as the source of power, through their elected representatives; (2) gave the council the right to enact laws concerning the state's income and expenditures, justice, public security, education, public health, public improvements, emergency, and whatever other laws might be necessary; (3) gave the council the power to review all treaties and concessions; (4) designated the council as a court of appeal until a special court was established; and (5) recognized the president of the council as the executive authority in the state.

7. The members (with the number of votes they received) were Yusuf ibn 'Isa (333), Hamad al-Marzuq (275), Khalid al-'Abd al-Latif (270), Mish'an al-Khudayr (265), Muhammad ibn Shahin (258), Sultan al-Kulayb (254), 'Abdullah al-Saqr (252), Mishari al-Hasan (250), 'Abd al-Latif al-Thunayan (248), al-Sayyid 'Ali al-Sayyid Sulayman (248), Ahmad ibn Khamis (237), Yusuf al-Humaydi (233), 'Ali al-Banwan (209), Sulayman al-'Adsani (205), Salih al-'Uthman (204), 'Ali al-'Abd al-Wahhab (202), Mishari al-Hilal

(198), Muhammad al-Ahmad al-Ghanim (185), Nusf ibn Yusuf (172), and Yusuf al-'Adsani (169).

8. In a final footnote, Ibn Sa'ud intervened on behalf of the imprisoned members, who were released on April 24, 1944. Muhammad al-Barrak, whose flogging had begun the 1938–1939 episode, was viewed with suspicion by the British during World War II for his alleged involvement with the Nazis in Iraq and Syria and with the Italians in India. The French deported him from Syria in 1940. He was arrested in India in 1941 and held there until returned to Kuwait in 1946.

9. The members were Shaykh 'Abdullah al-Salim (president), Shaykh Salim al-Hamud, Shaykh Fahd al-Salim, Shaykh 'Abdullah al-Jabir, Khalid al-Zayd al-Khalid, Muhammad ibn Shamlan, 'Abd al-Rahman Salim al-'Abd al-Razzaq, Thunayan al-Ghanim, Mishari al-Rudan, Muhammad al-Hamud al-Shay', and Ahmad al-Humaydi.

10. Public Record Office, London Foreign Office (FO) records, FO/371/109815, Sir Bernard Burrows, Political Resident in the Persian Gulf (PRPG), to Sir Anthony Eden, Secretary of State for Foreign Affairs, October 25, 1954.

11. 'Abdullah's official position was head of the security department but, more important, he was the only living son of Shaykh Mubarak the Great, acting ruler when the amir was abroad, implacable foe of reforms, and a potential claimant to the throne himself.

12. FO/371/109810, "Reports on Kuwait Administration and Subversion (1954)."

13. Al-Khatib was one of the first poor Kuwaitis to benefit from the implementation of Kuwait's social welfare policies in the 1950s. As a medical student at the American University of Beirut, he became one of the original officers of the Arab Nationalists' Movement (ANM), and on his return to Kuwait as the amirate's first native physician, he joined the Health Department, established a medical clinic, and founded an ANM branch, *Sada al-Iman*, and the National Cultural Club. He apparently became close to the present heir apparent, Shaykh Sa'd al-'Abdullah, when both were studying in the United Kingdom and was said to have turned down a cabinet portfolio in 1985. Walid Kazziha, *Revolutionary Transformation in the Arab World* (London: Charles Knight, 1975); Crystal, "Patterns of State-Building," 190; *al-Wa-*

tan (Kuwait), February 28, 1985; FO/371/114588, EA1017/16, C. J. Pelly, Political Agent, Kuwait (PAK), to Bernard Burrows, PRPG, June 7, 1955.

14. FO/371/114577, EA1013/8, "Monthly Summary of Events in the Persian Gulf for June 1955"; FO/371/114588, "Internal Political Situation in Kuwait," EA1017/16.

15. Ibid., EA1017/34, Gawain Bell, PAK, to D. M. H. Riches, FO Eastern Department, November 6, 1955.

16. FO/317/120540, EA1011/1, "Persian Gulf Annual Report for 1955," and FO/371/120541, "Monthly Summaries for the Persian Gulf for 1956"; and FO/371/120550, EA1017/14, Bell to Riches, April 17, 1956. Another initial function of the family council appeared to have been to consider appointment of a successor to Shaykh 'Abdullah. Because the appointment of a chairman would have implied his right to succeed, the Supreme Council never had a permanent chairman. The council's original members were Shaykhs 'Abdullah al-Mubarak, 'Abdullah al-Ahmad, Fahd al-Salim, Sabah al-Salim, Mubarak al-Hamad, Jabir al-Ahmad, Jabir al-'Ali, Sabah al-Ahmad, and Sa'd al-'Abdullah.

17. FO/371/120540, EA1011/1, "Persian Gulf Annual Report for 1955"; and FO/371/120541, "Monthly Summaries for the Persian Gulf for 1956."

18. Hashim, "The Influence of Iraq," 285–296. A series of raids carried out on May 6, 1956 resulted in the arrest of a number of alleged Communists of Iraqi, Iranian, and other nationalities. FO/371/120540, EA1011/1, "Persian Gulf Annual Report for 1955"; FO/371/120541, EA1013/9, "Monthly Report of Events in the Persian Gulf for May 1956."

19. FO/371/120541, Monthly Summaries for the Persian Gulf for 1956; FO/371/120551, EA1017/41, Kuwait Diary, no. 11, October 28 to November 28, 1956; and FO/120557, EA10113/45, Bell to Burrows, November 15, 1956.

20. Hashim, "The Influence of Iraq," 430–432.

21. On the National Assembly in Kuwait, see Aruri, "Kuwait"; Baz, "Political Elite"; Abdo I. Baaklini, "Legislatures in the Gulf Area: The Experience of Kuwait, 1961–1976," *International Journal of Middle East Studies* 14, no. 3 (1982), 359–379; Jassim Muhammad Khalaf, "The Kuwait National Assembly: A Study of Its Structure and Function" (unpublished Ph.D. dissertation, State University of New York, Albany, 1984); and Ghanim Hamad al-Najjar, "Decision-Making Process in Kuwait: The Land Acqui-

sition Policy as a Case Study" (unpublished Ph.D. thesis, University of Exeter, January 1984).

22. Baz discusses the constituent assembly and the constitution on pp. 148–169 and reproduces the text of the constitution on pp. 256–291. Dr. 'Uthman Khalil 'Uthman, an Egyptian expert in constitutional law, was the document's principal drafter.

23. According to the Kuwaiti electoral law, suffrage is denied to male Kuwaitis under the age of 21, women, military personnel, and citizens naturalized fewer than 20 years.

24. Baz, "Political Elite," 197–198.

25. Aruri, "Kuwait," 331. By one source, 100,000 to 200,000 bedouin from the Saudi or Iraqi members of the 'Ajman, Shammar, and Mutayr tribes were naturalized in the 1960s and 1970s to provide electoral support for the government. *The Middle East*, no. 69 (July 1980), 32, which also notes that the addition at the last minute of 500 bedouin to the electoral rolls in a district with 5,000 voters would be enough to influence the election outcome.

26. Aruri, "Kuwait," 335–337; Baz, "Political Elite," 187–193.

27. Aruri, "Kuwait," 338–339; Baz, "Political Elite," 193–194.

28. Interviews in Kuwait.

29. Baz, "Political Elite," 194–196.

30. Ibid., 214–220; *Middle East Annual Review 1977*, 215; J. E. Peterson, "Kuwait, Soviet Activities, and Gulf Security," in Z. Michael Szaz, ed., *The Impact of the Iranian Events Upon Persian Gulf and United States Security* (Washington, D.C.: American Foreign Policy Institute, 1979), 72–73. Baaklini, "Legislatures in the Gulf Area," 374, suggests that the formation of opposition groups in terms of friendship networks instead of formal political parties encouraged a tendency for groups to outbid each other with extreme positions, leading to a polarization of politics and confrontation, rather than compromise. Nicolas Gavriliedes maintains that the Al Sabah suspended the assembly as a result of the disintegration of a Sunni fundamentalist, Shi'a, and tribal alliance. "Tribal Democracy: The Anatomy of Parliamentary Elections in Kuwait," in Linda L. Layne, ed., *Elections in the Middle East: Implications of Recent Trends* (Boulder, Colo.: Westview Press, 1987, Westview Special Studies on the Middle East), 164.

31. Gavrielides, "Tribal Democracy," holds that the redistricting increased the seats in tribal areas from 25 to 31 and decreased the seats in Shi'a areas from 10 to 4, while the areas of predomi-

nantly urbanized Kuwaitis (*hadar*) retained 15 seats. Morocco provides another example of the sophistication of Middle Eastern monarchies in "fine-tuning" elections to achieve desirable results; see Dale Eickelman, "Royal Authority and Religious Legitimacy: Morocco's Elections, 1960-1984," in Myron J. Aronoff, ed., *The Frailty of Authority* (New Brunswick, N.J.: Transaction Books, 1986), 181-205.

32. *Economist*, February 28, 1981. Reasons advanced for the poor showing of Shi'a included discrimination in redistricting and schisms within the Shi'a community on ethnic (Arabs vs. Persians) and ideological (Islamics vs. establishment) lines. Shi'a had won 6 seats in 1963, 8 in 1967, 6 in 1971, and 10 in 1975. Khalaf, "The Kuwait National Assembly," 103. Khalaf puts the number of Shi'i winners in 1981 at four, while Gavrielides, "Tribal Democracy," 165, puts their numbers at five. Gavrielidies also gives the total of bedouin as 27 (p. 165), although his chart listing the National Assembly members (pp. 187-188) lists only 23 bedouin. For background on some of the assembly's members, see Khalaf, "The Kuwait National Assembly," 128-135.

33. Gavrielides points out that the existing organizational structure of the tribes allowed them to reach consensus on suitable candidates to represent the tribe through formal primaries, an option not viable for the other political blocs, which lack proper organization because of the ban on political parties. "Tribal Democracy," 168. He concludes that the primaries allow the tribes "to use tribal ideology to solidify their membership and provide their members with a meaningful group identity that relates to the formal political process and structure." Ibid., 170. The state welcomes this type of political participation because it both exemplifies the regime's ideology and strengthens the sectors of the electorate most supportive of the regime.

34. *Arab Times* (Kuwait), February 23, 1985; *Middle East International*, March 8, 1985; and *Middle East Economic Digest*, Special Report on Kuwait, April 1985. Gavrielides, "Tribal Democracy," asserts that four Shi'a were elected in 1985 (p. 179). The discrepancy appears to have arisen from his identification of Salim al-Hammad as Shi'i in his list of the 1985 candidates (p. 209). But Hammad is noted as being from the 'Azimi tribe in Gavrielides' reproduction of Nafisi's cumulative list of assembly members (p. 202), which is the same identification as given in 'Abdul-

lah Fahd al-Nafisi, *al-Kuwayt: al-Ra'i al-Akhir* (London: Ta-Ha Advertising, 1978), 89.

35. By custom though not law, members of the Al Sabah are excluded from voting and from elected membership in the National Assembly. This informal prohibition on participation by ruling families is evident in all the elected and appointed assemblies in the Gulf. At least one Al Sabah is reported to have voted in the 1985 election, however, and an Al Khalifa was elected to the 1973–1975 Bahraini National Assembly. For the election platforms of Kuwaiti political groups, see al-Nafisi, *al-Kuwayt*.

36. For detail on the group's organization and aims, as well as the defection of some members, see the *Arab Times*, December 9, 10, 11, 1985, and January 11, 1986. Tribalists won 19 seats in 1963, 20 in 1967 and 1971, 21 in 1975, and 27 in 1981. Khalaf, "The Kuwait National Assembly," 103. The tribal impact on Kuwaiti elections is discussed in Nafisi, *al-Kuwayt*, 78–90, along with a complete list of election winners by district and ethnic or tribal affiliation for the period 1963–1975. See also Gavrielides, "Tribal Democracy."

37. One visible indicator of neoconservatism in Kuwait is evident in dress. Many young women have adopted the *hijab* or Islamic style of dress. Within the National Assembly, the number of members wearing Western suits has declined from as many as 20 in the mid-1970s to 2 in the mid-1980s. Invariably, these two were secularized leftist leader Ahmad al-Khatib and 'Abd al-Rahman al-Ghunaym, a secularized former government official, pro-government assembly member, and, since July 1986, a cabinet member.

38. The only Shi'a in the February 1985 cabinet was 'Isa Muhammad al-Mazidi, who had first entered the cabinet in 1981 after election to the National Assembly. In the July 1986 cabinet, al-Mazidi was demoted to minister of state for services affairs, al-Khurafi was retained and 'Abd al-Rahman al-Ghunaym (a former under secretary in the Ministry of Communications) was recruited from the suspended National Assembly as minister of state for Municipal Affairs.

39. On the suspension, see the *Washington Post*, July 4, 1986; Wakalat al-Anba' al-Khalij (Manama) in English, July 5, 1986 (FBIS, Middle East and South Asia, July 8, 1986); *Middle East Economic Survey*, July 7, 1986; the *Economist*, July 12,

1986; *Defense and Foreign Affairs Weekly*, July 14–20, 1986; *The Middle East*, no. 142, August 1986; and Abdo I. Baaklini, "Dissolution of the Kuwait National Assembly," unpublished paper given at the annual conference of the Middle East Studies Association, Boston, November 23, 1986.

40. *Al-Watan*, November 12, 1985.

41. Text broadcast on Kuwait Domestic Service, July 3, 1986 (FBIS, Middle East and Africa, July 7, 1986).

42. John Whelan, ed., *Kuwait: A MEED Practical Guide* (London: Middle East Economic Digest, 1985), 90–91; S. M. Al-Sabah, *Kuwait: Anatomy of a Crisis Economy* (London: Eastlords Publishing, 1984), 6–12; Jasim al-Sa'dun, *Manakh al-Azma wa-Azmat al-Manakh* (Kuwait: Sharikat al-Rubayyi'an lil-Nashr wal-Tawzi', 1984); and Fida Darwiche, *The Gulf Stock Exchange Crash: The Rise and Fall of the Souq al-Manakh* (London: Croom Helm, 1986). Suq al-Manakh is a modern shopping mall in Kuwait City, built on the site of a resting place for camel caravans and across the street from the new Kuwait Stock Exchange.

43. *Al-Watan*, August 15, 1983; Whelan, *Kuwait*, 90–91; *Middle East Economic Digest*, December 7, 1985; *Arab Times*, January 7 and 19, 1986; *Middle East Economic Survey*, July 14, 1986.

44. *Al-Watan* and *Arab Times*, May 6, 1985.

45. Previous terrorist activities had included the bombing of the U.S. and French embassies, as well as various government installations, in December 1983; the hijacking of a Kuwaiti airliner to Tehran in December 1984; an assassination attempt on the amir in May 1985; and the bombing of two seaside cafes in July 1985. Subsequently, terrorists set off more explosions in the oilfields and a car bomb exploded in downtown Kuwait City on the eve of the Islamic summit conference in January 1987.

46. Text of July 3, 1986 address to the nation published in *al-Watan*, July 4, 1986 (FBIS, July 7, 1986).

47. Law Decree No. 30 for 1986, October 18, 1986, text in *Majallat Dirasat al-Khalij wal-Jazira al-'Arabiya* 13, no. 49 (January 1987), 244–245.

48. Khalaf, "The Kuwait National Assembly," 153–185, discusses the assembly's structure, committees, and formal functions.

49. *Al-Watan*, June 24 and July 18, 1985; *Arab Times*, July

13, 1985; *Gulf States Newsletter*, July 29, 1985; and interviews in Kuwait.

50. Interviews in Kuwait.

51. *Arab Times*, December 11, 18, and 25, 1985.

52. The cabinets formed in the middle of this period consistently had only five Al Sabah members, except for that of February 1971, which reduced the royal contingent to three. Baaklini, "Legislatures in the Gulf Area," 367.

53. Khalaf, "The Kuwait National Assembly," 135–139; and Abdo I. Baaklini, "The Kuwaiti Legislature as Ombudsman: The Legislative Committee on Petitions and Complaints," *Legislative Studies Quarterly* 3, no. 2 (May 1978), 293–307.

54. *Arab Times*, November 27 and 30, December 1 and 4, 1985.

55. *Arab Times*, December 8, 15, and 30, 1985. For some, criticism of the admissions policy appeared to be part of the Islamics' disguised attack on the liberal and relatively secularized minister of education.

56. The information in this section is based on *Arab Times*, February 20 and 21, 1984; *Washington Post*, April 14, 1984; *New York Times*, December 17, 1984; *al-Safir* (Beirut), February 18, 1985; *The Middle East*, no. 132 (October 1985): 7–9; and interviews in Kuwait.

Chapter 3

1. On the historical and social background to Bahrain, see Ahmad Mustafa Abu Hakima, *History of Eastern Arabia, 1750–1800: The Rise and Development of Bahrain and Kuwait* (Beirut: Khayats, 1965); M. G. Rumaihi, *Bahrain: Social and Political Change Since the First World War* (London: Bowker, 1976, in association with the Centre for Middle Eastern and Islamic Studies of the University of Durham); Fuad I. Khuri, *Tribe and State in Bahrain: The Transformation of Social and Political Authority in an Arab State* (Chicago: University of Chicago Press, 1980); and Talal Toufic Farah, *Protection and Politics in Bahrain, 1869–1915* (Beirut: American University of Beirut, 1985).

2. The following section is based on Muhammad al-Rumayhi, "Harakat 1938 al-islahi fi al-Kuwayt wa-al-Bahrayn wa-Dubayy," *Majallat dirasat al-Khalij wa-al-Jazira al-'Arabiya* 1, no. 4 (Octo-

ber 1975): 29–68; idem, *Bahrain*; Khuri, *Tribe and State in Bahrain;* Saeed Khalil Hashim, "The Influence of Iraq on the Nationalist Movements of Kuwait and Bahrain, 1920–1961" (unpublished Ph.D. dissertation, University of Exeter, March 1984); documents in the India Office Library and Records (IOLR; London), especially L/P&S/18/B396, "Bahrein, 1908–1928," by J. G. Laithwaite (October 8, 1928); L/P&S/B420, "Question of British Interference in the Administration of Bahrein," despatch from the Political Resident in the Persian Gulf to the Foreign Secretary to the Government of India, August 28, 1929; L/P&S/12/3719 and L/P&S/12/3720A, "Persian Gulf Annual Administration Reports," 1926–1945; R/15/2/83, "Tyranny of the Ruling Family in Bahrain" (1921–1923); R/15/2/312 and R/15/2/313, "Bahrain Intelligence Summaries" (1935–1940); and Foreign Office (FO) records in the Public Record Office (PRO; London), especially FO/371/104260, FO/371/109806, FO/371/114576, FO/371/114577, FO/371/120540, and FO/371/120541, "Annual and Monthly Summaries of Events in the Persian Gulf," 1952–1956; FO/371/104263, "Disturbances in Bahrain (September 1953)"; FO/371/114586, FO/371/114587, and FO/371/120544–120549, "Internal Political Situation in Bahrain" (1954–1956).

3. A board of inquiry into the causes of the market shooting reported that the police, without orders, fired nearly 500 rounds into the crowd, killing 5 and wounding 12. Nevertheless, it added that the police had been under considerable provocation and that at least one of those killed had been hit by a bullet from a non-police revolver. No charges were brought against the policemen involved, but the ruler later announced that he would pay compensation to the victims.

4. The ruler objected to the name HEC, because it connoted a rival or even superior authority. The Kuwaiti government used the same term in the 1950s for its quasi-cabinet.

5. The council, the predecessor of today's cabinet, was charged with coordinating the administration of the various departments, expediting the conduct of government business, receiving communications from the public and acting on their grievances, taking care to inform the public of government decisions; allocation of state revenue and foreign affairs were specifically excluded from the council's jurisdiction. Among the 10 members, appointed for one-year terms, were Shaykh 'Abdullah ibn 'Isa Al Khalifa, the ruler's uncle; Shaykh Da'ij ibn Hamad Al Khalifa,

younger brother of the ruler and a potential successor; Shaykh Khalifa ibn Muhammad, a nephew of the ruler; Shaykh Khalid ibn Muhammad ibn 'Abdullah, a nephew of Shaykh 'Abdullah ibn 'Isa; Ahmad 'Umran, the director of education and a staunch supporter of the ruler; Salim al-'Urayyid, a Shi'i official in the Judicial Department; and G. W. R. Smith, director of customs and the port.

6. The British attitude to the opposition movement underwent an abrupt reversal in late 1956, apparently in response to the Arab reaction to Suez. From an early date, Sir Bernard Burrows, the British Political Resident in the Persian Gulf (PRPG), had recognized the need to keep on good terms with both sides, preferably by agreeing with the necessity of reasonable reforms, negotiating between the reformers and the ruler, and by pushing the ruler into making these reforms. The ruler and Belgrave had contemplated arresting the HEC/CNU leaders as early as the March 1955 events, but were dissuaded from doing so for fear of causing additional disturbances and by the British, who were unwilling to provide armed forces in support and who counseled concessions instead. Both Burrows and the Foreign Office agreed that Belgrave's departure was desirable but they were reluctant to say so publicly or to push either the ruler or Belgrave. In a March 1956 report on the political situation in Bahrain, Burrows noted that

> Bahrain is going through a period of constitutional and political development which on the whole is taking what history shows to be a fairly normal course. The Ruler is seeking to give away as little as possible for fear of his own future while reformists press on with increasing enthusiasm. . . . The position of the British Government is delicate [but] as a democratic government it cannot disapprove of or repress those aspirations of the people of Bahrain, expressed through the Committee, which are reasonable, as many of them are. And the Committee through conviction and intimidation can in fact mobilize widespread support.

(FO/371/120541, EA1013/8, untitled ["Secret"] report from PRPG on March 1956 disturbances in Bahrain, n.d.)

A few months later, the British attitude had changed. In September, Burrows reported that the CNU appeared to be moving to a more extreme position and abandoning the constructive approach to constitutional development. Following the outbreak of the protest march against Suez in early November, Burrows wrote that while the decision to suppress the CNU was entirely that of the Bahraini government, he saw no reason to advise against it. A few weeks later, he added that he felt that the CNU seemed to be moving fairly rapidly towards adopting the violent overthrow of the government as its aim.

7. The most serious evidence was a document addressed to "The Free People of Bahrain" and signed by "The Commandos." Allegedly found in the possession of al-'Ulaywat, the document was said to assert that future operations would include the assassination of the ruler, his adviser, and other members of the ruling family, as well as the burning of the ruler's palace, the airport, and some foreign buildings. Al-Bakir was said to have mentioned blowing up foreign buildings in a speech in Beirut, thus linking him to the document. The government produced letters to Colonel Anwar al-Sadat, then an Egyptian minister of state, written by al-Shamlan but not mailed, containing such incriminating statements as that the purpose of the CNU was the "setting up of a Legislative Assembly to reduce the powers of the Ruler" and that the CNU "aims at putting an end to the powers of the feudalistic ruler." Al-Shamlan's request in one of those letters for Egyptian President Jamal 'Abd al-Nasir to disregard a letter from the Bahraini ruler – a letter which in fact was never sent – was cited as an intention to influence a foreign government against the wishes of the ruler of Bahrain. The defendants were also charged with creating disorder because they had accepted responsibility for holding a "peaceful" procession and it had ended in voilence and destruction.

8. John Duke Anthony, *Arab States of the Lower Gulf: People, Politics, Petroleum* (Washington, D.C.: Middle East Institute, 1975), 47–49; and *Fiches du Monde Arabe* (FMA), no. 1605, June 11, 1980.

9. Emile A. Nakhleh, *Bahrain: Political Development in a Modernizing Society* (Lexington, Mass.: Lexington, Books/D.C. Heath, 1976), 125, notes the emphasis of the ruler during these discussions that the issuance of a constitution was neither a response to popular demand nor an extension of popular sovereignty. Rather, the Al Khalifa viewed the proposed national assembly as a modification of the traditional principle of *shura*, which in no way restricted their legitimate right to rule. A series of interviews

on what people wanted in a constitution, published by *al-Adwa'* (Manama) in 1972, are summarized in ibid., 118–124.

10. On the election, see Nakhleh, *Bahrain*, 133–164, including a list of the assembly's members on pp. 163–164. It is striking how the same names frequently crop up at different times. For example, 'Abd al-'Aziz al-Shamlan's father, Sa'd, was exiled to India as a result of his involvement in the 1938 events. Ahmad al-Shirawi, the other 1938 leader exiled to India and who later settled in Saudi Arabia, was the father of Bahrain's current minister of development and industry, Yusuf al-Shirawi. 'Abd 'Ali al-'Ulaywat, an activist in 1938, was exiled to St. Helena in 1956, while Ibrahim Fakhru, also an activist in 1938, was one of the two CNU leaders imprisoned in Bahrain in 1956. Hasan al-Jishi, arrested in 1956 and exiled to Kuwait, was elected speaker of the National Assembly in 1973.

11. Ibid., 142–143, including the text of the petition on pp. 143–144.

12. FMA, no. 1605, June 11, 1980; and Emile A. Nakhleh, *The Persian Gulf and American Policy* (New York, N.Y.: Praeger, 1982), 28–32.

13. Nakhleh, *Bahrain*, 126–127.

14. The text of the constitution is contained in John N. Gatch, Jr., "Bahrain," in Albert P. Blaustein and Gisbert H. Flanz, eds., *Constitutions of the Countries of the World* (Dobbs Ferry, N.Y.: Oceana Publications, December 1974), 1–31.

15. FMA, no. 1605, June 11, 1980; Khuri, *Tribe and States in Bahrain*, 218–233; Emile A. Nakhleh, "Political Participation and the Constitutional Experiments in the Arab Gulf: Bahrain and Qatar," in Tim Niblock, ed., *Social and Economic Development in the Arab Gulf* (London: Croom Helm, for the University of Exeter Centre for Arab Gulf Studies, 1980), 161–176; and idem, *The Persian Gulf and American Policy*, 21–41 (including a list of the elected members on p. 33).

16. Nakhleh, "Political Participation," 168, notes the importance of the election's timing in producing such a large leftist contingent (occurring shortly after the October 1973 war and in the midst of the Arab oil embargo), as well as the regime's decision to permit a remarkably free election.

17. Interviews in Bahrain.

18. Khuri, *Tribe and State*, 225–226, notes that the high Shi'i

religious establishment considered themselves to be custodians of the "rights" of all the people. Therefore, they could not subject their authority to elections, anymore than the Al Khalifa, having earned the right to rule through heredity, could submit to the vagaries of public opinion.

19. Many leading families remained aloof from the elections on grounds that they were either too busy with business or because they regarded the process of standing for election as undignified. *Financial Times* (London), May 31, 1983.

20. Initially, the ministry could detain an individual for six months, after which the prisoner could appeal to the High Appeal Court. In the absence of an appeal, the ministry could go before the court and ask for an additional three-months detention, which was almost automatically approved. By law, this could be repeated for a total period of up to three years. Interviews in Bahrain.

21. Interviews in Bahrain.

22. Much of this section is based on interviews in Bahrain in 1980 and 1986.

23. Interviews in Bahrain.

24. It is widely assumed outside of Bahrain that Iran's revolution and the war with Iraq have worked to increase Sunni-Shi'i tensions, and reference has been made to several Shi'i demonstrations, in particular the anti-Iraq riots in April 1980 against Iraq's execution of its leading Shi'i figure, Ayatollah Muhammad Baqir al-Sadr. But Shi'i support for Iran slackened in the months after the revolution as the result of the abortive renewal of Iran's claim to the amirate, the Iranian threat to kill the (Arab Shi'i) Khuzistanis occupying the Iranian embassy in London, and especially the excesses of the new republican regime. More fundamentally, recent socioeconomic developments have helped to break down the traditional geographic and social divisions separating the sects. The fall in agricultural employment to about 1 percent of the population has sparked rural migration to the towns. The sects are mixed in new settlements such as al-'Adliya, al-Qudaybiya, Umm al-Hasam, 'Isa Town, and Hamad Town, and there is more socialization between Sunnis and Shi'a in such areas as schools and government employment. These positive developments are undercut however, by the political indoctrination of mullas in the Shi'i ma'tam and the hostile attitudes of Jami'at al-Islah (the Muslim Brotherhood). Although the sectarian split of the population not surprisingly is a closely held secret, probably

60 percent of Bahrainis are Shi'a, with al-Manama approximately 65 percent Sunni and Muharraq mostly Sunni. Interviews in Bahrain.

25. Interviews in Bahrain. Although it was conceded that a consultative council might appear attractive to conservative elements in the Al Khalifa and in the government, there was concern that Bahrainis would not accept such a council because it would seem regressive compared with the previous National Assembly. In addition, it was felt that reduction to a consultative council would be an embarrassment, given the longer existence of consultative councils in less-developed Qatar and the UAE. In the end, the reluctance of the government to encourage public discussion of even a council was regarded as fear that it would capture popular enthusiasm and thus force the government's hand.

26. Interviews in Bahrain; Nakhleh, *The Persian Gulf and American Policy*, 36. Nakhleh suggests various clusters of opinion have emerged regarding the National Assembly: a moderate group within the ruling family, represented by Shaykh Muhammad ibn Mubarak; a middle class, liberal view, represented by businessman Jasim Murad; the leftist bloc, led by 'Ali Rabi'a; and a cautious approach by the conservative Shi'a religious establishment. Ibid., 37–38.

27. Interviews in Bahrain.

28. *al-Mawaqif*, no. 558, February 25, 1985.

29. *Sada al-Usbu'*, February 26, 1985.

Chapter 4

1. As Emile Nakhleh notes, "Qatar has experienced neither the euphoria of drafting, ratifying and promulgating a constitution, nor the trauma of the failure of such a constitution. Generally speaking, the al-Thani ruling family in Qatar has not supported the more liberal trends of its al-Khalifa counterpart in Bahrain. Furthermore, compared to Bahrain, Qatar has had a smaller population, a more limited level of education and a much more recent labour tradition. Being part of the Arabian desert mainland, Qatar has not experienced as much interaction with other cultures as has the island country of Bahrain. In addition, Qatar has not had a politically conscious class of urban intelligentsia, as is the case in Bahrain." Nakhleh, "Political Participation and the Constitutional Experiments in the Arab Gulf: Bahrain and Qatar," in Tim

Niblock, ed., *Social and Economic Development in the Arab Gulf* (London: Croom Helm, for the University of Exeter Centre for Arab Gulf Studies, 1980), 170–171.

2. For general background on the State of Qatar, see Muhammad T. Sadik and William P. Snavely, *Bahrain, Qatar, and the United Arab Emirates: Colonial Past, Present Problems, and Future Prospects* (Lexington, Mass.: Lexington Books/D.C. Heath, 1972); John Duke Anthony, *Arab States of the Lower Gulf: People, Politics, Petroleum* (Washington, D.C.: Middle East Institute, 1975); Rosemarie Said Zahlan, *The Creation of Qatar* (London: Croom Helm; New York: Barnes & Noble, 1979); Yousof Ibrahim Al-Abdulla, *A Study of Qatari-British Relations, 1914–1945* (Doha: Orient Publishing and Translation, n.d. [1982?]); Zuhair Ahmed Nafi, *Economic and Social Development in Qatar* (London: Frances Pinter, 1984); Nasser al-Othman, *With Their Bare Hands: The Story of the Oil Industry in Qatar* (London: Longman, 1984; tr. and ed. by Ken Whittingham); Ragaei El Mallakh, *Qatar: Energy and Development* (London: Croom Helm, 1985); State of Qatar, Ministry of Information, Press and Publications Department, *Year Book, 1982–83* (Doha, n.d. [1985?]); and Jill Crystal, "Patterns of State-Building in the Arabian Gulf: Kuwait and Qatar" (unpublished Ph.D. dissertation, Harvard University, 1986).

3. The council was established by Law 6 of May 6, 1964, as published in *al-Jarida al-Rasmiya*, no. 3, May 6, 1964. Its membership is given in Decree 5 of May 13, 1964, as published in *al-Jarida al-Rasmiya*, no. 4, May 20, 1964.

4. "The Provisional Constitution for the State of Qatar," April 2, 1970; "The Amended Provisional Constitution of the State of Qatar," April 19, 1972. The numbering of articles in the following discussion refers to the amended constitution except where otherwise noted.

5. Material on the council is drawn primarily from the State of Qatar, Advisory Council, *The Advisory Council in Brief* (prepared by Qusai al-Abadleh, in Arabic and English; tr. by Fawzi Abdulilah; Doha, 1401/1981); and from interviews with members of the council, the secretariat, and other Qataris in Doha.

6. The constitution stipulates that council members must be original Qatari citizens, not less than 24 years old, and not convicted of breach of honor (unless rehabilitated according to the

law) (Art. 42). They also must be of respectable social standing, of good judgment, and of competence in various fields (Art. 43).

7. This breakdown of members adds up to only 29, due to a vacant seat that had not been filled as of mid-1987. Qatar's small Shi'a community is probably over-represented, with at least one if not two members.

8. Officials in Qatar justified the inclusion of government officials in the council by pointing to the example of Egypt's parliament. At the same time, they acknowledge that Kuwait prevents this "double role" and concede that Kuwait had the most advanced parliament in the Arab world.

9. There are four kinds of legal authority in Qatar, all subject to the amir's control. In order of precedence, these are (1) the constitution, (2) laws or decree laws, (3) decrees, and (4) internal regulations. Decree laws are laws signed by the amir when the council is not in session and are binding only until considered by the council at its first session. Decrees are used mostly for administrative matters or the establishment of a company and cannot be issued for relatively serious matters, such as establishing a tax or for imprisonment. Internal regulations concern the internal matters of a ministry or other agency, for example.

10. Inquiries may be of two types. General discussion requests must be presented by five or more members and are concerned with general subjects, such as the condition of education in general, rather than a request for a particular school, or a complaint on the cost of living. Private member's requests can be brought up by a single member and would be a request for the government to do something, such as build a school or reduce the price of electricity. Such a request is routed through the appropriate committee of the council and then the council itself before being raised with the appropriate ministry or minister.

11. For basic background on the Trucial States and the UAE, see Sadik and Snavely, *Bahrain, Qatar, and the United Arab Emirates*; Anthony, *Arab States of the Lower Gulf*; Rosemarie Said Zahlan, *The Origins of the United Arab Emirates: A Political and Social History of the Trucial States* (London: Macmillan, 1978); Ali Mohammed Khalifa, *The United Arab Emirates: Unity in Fragmentation* (Boulder, Colo.: Westview Press; London: Croom Helm, 1979); Frauke Heard-Bey, *From Trucial States to United Arab Emirates: A Society in Transition* (London:

142 Political Participation in the Arab Gulf States

Longman, 1983); Abdulkhaleq Abdulla, "Political Dependency:
The Case of the United Arab Emirates" (unpublished Ph.D. dis-
sertation, Georgetown University, 1984); Muhammad Salih al-
Musfir, "The United Arab Emirates: An Assessment of Federal-
ism in a Developing Polity" (unpublished Ph.D. dissertation,
State University of New York at Binghamton, 1984); Malcolm
Peck, *The United Arab Emirates: A Venture in Unity* (Boulder,
Colo.: Westview Press; London: Croom Helm, 1986); and Naomi
Sakr, *The United Arab Emirates to the 1990s: One Market or
Seven?* (London: Economist Intelligence Unit, March 1986, Spe-
cial Report, no. 238).

12. The text of the constitution is contained in Amos J. Peaslee,
Constitutions of Nations, vol. 2, pt. 2, rev. 4th ed. (Dordrecht:
Martinus Nijhoff Publishers, 1985), 1700–1724.

13. Rosemarie Said Zahlan, "Hegemony, Dependence and Devel-
opment in the Gulf," in Tim Niblock, ed., *Social and Economic
Development in the Arab Gulf* (London: Croom Helm, for the
University of Exeter Centre for Arab Gulf Studies, 1980), 66.
Zahlan also notes that these relatively prosperous centers at-
tracted considerable migration from neighboring areas, e.g., from
Qatar to Bahrain and from Sharjah to Dubai.

14. On the 1938 movement, see Rosemarie J. Said, "The 1938
Reform Movement in Dubai," *Al-Abhath* 23, nos. 1–4 (December
1970): 247–318; Muhammad al-Rumayhi, "Harakat 1938 al-islahi
fi al-Kuwayt wa-al-Bahrayn wa-Dubayy," *Majallat dirasat al-Khalij wa-al-Jazira al-'Arabiya* 1, no. 4 (October 1975): 29–68; Heard-
Bey, *From Trucial States to United Arab Emirates*, 252–258;
and the India Office Library and Records (IOLR; London), especially L/P&S/12/3720A, "Persian Gulf Annual Administration
Reports, 1939–1945"; and R/15/2/1882, "Dubai Reforms."
Rosemarie Said (Zahlan) includes in her article the Arabic texts of
the correspondence between the reform leaders, the ruler, and the
British Residency Agent in Sharjah, transcribed from IOLR,
R/15/2/1882.

15. To defuse tensions, the Rashid cousins were induced
to leave Sharjah for Hamasa in the Buraimi oasis. In October
1939, Shaykh Sa'id accused five persons of plotting to aid the
Rashid in returning to Dubai and had their eyes gouged out.
The act caused strong revulsion and facilitated the return of
the Rashid to Sharjah in early 1940. The refusal of the ruler of
Sharjah to turn them out nearly brought the neighboring shaykh-

doms into conflict before a truce was arranged. Mani' ibn Rashid, the most prominent of the opposition figures, eventually moved to Bombay.

16. Public Record Office, London; Foreign Office Records (FO), FO/371/114577, EA1013/4, Monthly Summary of Events in the Persian Gulf, March 1955; FO/1016/455, "Dubai Affairs" (1955); FO/371/120541, EA1013/14 and EA/1013/15, "Monthly Summaries of Events in the Persian Gulf for August and September 1956"; and FO/371/120553, EA1019/6, J. P. Tripp, Political Agent in the Trucial States, to Charles Gault, Political Residency in the Persian Gulf, June 28, 1956. Tripp provided biographical information on 29 National Front members, including founders Ahmad ibn Sultan ibn Sulayyim and Hamid ibn Majid ibn Ghurayr. The list included Shaykh Juma and various members of the Ibn Ghurayr and Ibn Futayyim merchant families.

17. Information on national councils in the UAE was gathered from Anthony, *Arab States of the Lower Gulf*; Heard-Bey, *From Trucial States to United Arab Emirates*; Khalifa, *The United Arab Emirates*; interviews in the UAE; and various UAE newspapers.

18. For example, Dubai is represented by members of such well-known merchant families as Luta, Ghurayr, and Kaytub; similarly, Sharjah is represented by Madfa' and Jarwan and Ra's al-Khayma by Ghubash (until 1985) and Shal. Abu Dhabi's members include self-made businessmen who have held the franchises for BMW, Datsun, and GM, as well as a former banking official and the deputy director of Abu Dhabi municipality. Another was one of the first Abu Dhabians to be sent to Qatar for schooling and returned to be a schoolteacher before becoming head of the amirate's low-cost housing authority.

19. Tiryam is the publisher, and his brother Rashid the editor, of Sharjah's *al-Khalij*, a controversial, Nasirist newspaper that was banned for a number of years because of its radical views, and banned again briefly in 1987 during the abortive coup in Sharjah. Another brother, 'Abdullah, served as minister of education until he was dropped during a cabinet reshuffle in July 1979, supposedly because he was held responsible for student-led demonstrations calling for total unity within the federation.

20. *Al-Ittihad* (Abu Dhabi), January 15, 1984.

21. *Al-Bayan* (Dubai), June 18, 1983. Similarly, 9 federal laws and 3 federal decrees, all issued after the previous FNC had end-

ed, awaited the 1986–1987 FNC at its first sitting. *Khaleej Times* (Dubai), January 25, 1986.

22. *Khaleej Times* (Dubai), February 26 and March 12, 1986.

23. *Gulf News* (Dubai), June 23, 1983; *al-Ittihad* (Abu Dhabi), February 1, 1984 and January 9, 1985.

24. In one case, a government employee was reportedly fined 7,500 dirhams as a penalty for overstaying his visa. The problem was caused by the Immigration Department's regulation allowing 30 days to leave the country following the end of employment – while it took the employing agency 45 days to release him. *Khaleej Times* (Dubai), March 26, 1986.

25. As many of the NCC members live away from the amirate's urban centers in their tribal territories, the NCC probably has closer contact with the people than the FNC, whose members are drawn largely from established merchant families. *The Middle East*, no. 68 (June 1980): 29–30.

26. In this regard, for example, see the record of the NCC's complaints about government harassment of Abu Dhabi citizens and the bureaucracy's penchant for excessive regulation in the *Khaleej Times* (Dubai), March 3, 1986. NCC members' salary was adjusted in 1983 to 15,000 UAE dirhams per month. *Al-Bayan* (Dubai), May 27, 1983.

27. Interview with Shaykh Sultan, March 12, 1986.

28. In an interview, Shaykh 'Abd al-'Aziz declared that "the UAE issues laws. The emirate issues others. Therefore, the people should participate in discussing draft laws before their issuance. The people should be represented by a consultative council [of about 35 members] elected from notables of the emirate. These people should have a good reputation and the experience of their fathers." He suggested that the council might hear the cases of those accused of corruption. *Al-Qabas* (Kuwait), June 19, 1987 (FBIS, June 22, 1987).

29. Initially, 21 members were appointed by Amiri Decree 12/ 1987, which announced the establishment of the council in the context of a government reorganization. Wakalat al-Anba' al-Khalij (Manama), July 20, 1987 (FBIS, July 22, 1987). Another five members were appointed by Amiri Decree 13/1987, containing additional changes. Ibid., July 22, 1987 (FBIS, July 23, 1987).

30. Heard-Bey, *From Trucial States to United Arab Emirates*, 397–401.

31. Quoted in *The Middle East*, no. 68 (June 1980): 31.

32. For background on Oman, see Robert Geran Landen, *Oman Since 1856: Disruptive Modernization in a Traditional Arab Society* (Princeton, N.J.: Princeton University Press, 1967); Derek Hopwood, ed., *The Arabian Peninsula: Society and Politics* (London: George Allen & Unwin, 1972); John Townsend, *Oman: The Making of a Modern State* (London: Croom Helm; New York: St. Martin's Press, 1977); J. C. Wilkinson, *Water and Tribal Settlement in South-East Arabia* (Oxford: Clarendon Press, 1977); idem, *The Imamate Tradition of Oman* (Cambridge: Cambridge University Press, 1987); J. E. Peterson, *Oman in the Twentieth Century: Political Foundations of an Emerging State* (London: Croom Helm; New York: Barnes and Noble, 1978); and idem, "Legitimacy and Political Change in Yemen and Oman," *Orbis* 27, no. 4 (Winter 1984): 971–998.

33. Published information on the SCC is contained in Dale F. Eickelman, "Kings and People: Oman's State Consultative Council," *Middle East Journal* 38, no. 1 (Winter 1984): 51–71; and the Sultanate of Oman, *The State Consultative Council in Four Years* (Muscat, n.d. [1985?]). The following account also relies upon interviews in Muscat with SCC members, a former president, and cabinet ministers.

34. Eickelman, "Kings and People," 55, notes the role of the Council on Agriculture, Fisheries, and Industry, established in April 1979, in preparing the way for the later appearance of the SCC, specifically in drafting the first policy recommendations by a body "outside" the government and in gaining the support or at least neutrality of some government officials for the idea of consultation.

35. The social service ministries are Interior; Education, Guidance, and Youth Affairs; Health; Social Affairs and Labor; Housing; Municipalities; Commerce and Industry; Agriculture and Fisheries; Communications; Electricity and Water; and Post, Telegraph, and Telephone. In addition to government officials appointed because of their positions or standing, a number of other regional members have also been government employees. Members must be Omani nationals and at least 30 years old.

36. The president receives an annual salary of RO 20,000, while the two vice presidents each receive RO 15,000, and the other members RO 10,000 – except for government officials who receive only half that amount.

37. Eickelman, "Kings and People," 61–63.

38. Issues for discussion can be raised by the sultan, the cabinet, members of the SCC, and any two or more citizens. A matter raised by one citizen is handled privately by a SCC member or the Executive Committee on behalf of the citizen.

39. Eickelman, "Kings and People," 64, quotes one SCC member as explaining that "the committees are where our recommendations are 'cooked.' By the time issues are discussed in the full quarterly meetings, the major lines of recommendations have already been decided."

40. *The State Consultative Council in Four Years*, 24–32.

41. This apparently was the case with the proposal for the 500-bed hospital at al-Khula, near Muscat. Another aspect of this new policy is that the cabinet secretary must report to the SCC president on the council's recommendations, including what steps the cabinet took, the status of implementation in the appropriate ministry, or the status of incorporation into the five-year plan.

42. The first president was Khalfan Nasir al-Wuhaybi, who had been minister of labor and social affairs and returned to a position as minister of electricity and water. The second president was Hamud 'Abdullah al-Harithi, who had been minister of electricity and water and was returned to a position as minister of communications. The third president was Salim ibn Nasir Al Bu Sa'idi, formerly minister of communications.

Chapter 5

1. Public Record Office (PRO, London), Foreign Office (FO) records, FO/371/14577, EA1013/4, "Monthly Summary of Events in the Persian Gulf, March 1955." Of course, radical leftist and, more recently, equally radical Islamic groups have sought to replace regimes by radically different political systems, although none of these organizations appears to have enjoyed much support.

2. Khalid Ahmed Al-Shalal, "The Trade Union Movement in the State of Kuwait: A Sociohistorical and Analytical Study" (unpublished Ph.D. dissertation, Michigan State University, 1984), 99 and 102; and FO/371/109806, EA1013/1, "Monthly Summary of Events in the Persian Gulf, December 1953."

3. The strike was caused by the dismissal of a worker for incompetence and striking a foreman, and it was quickly ended

when 'Abd al-Rahman al-Bakir of the HEC told the strikers that the dismissal was justified and that they should return to work. FO/371/114577, EA1013/7, "Monthly Summary of Events in the Persian Gulf, May 1955."

4. FO/371/110095, "Annual Review for Saudi Arabia for 1953"; FO/371/104882, "Strike by Aramco Employees (1953)." An earlier strike at Ra's Tanura in 1945 was quickly put down by Turki ibn 'Utayshan, the formidable governor of the Eastern Province, who had his personal bodyguard seize the leaders and then he personally and publicly flogged them.

5. FO/371/114874, "Internal Political Events in Saudi Arabia (1955)", ES1015/7, H. Phillips, ambassador to Saudi Arabia, Jidda, to Harold Macmillan, foreign secretary, May 12, 1955; and H. Beeley, Jidda, to L. A. C. Fry, FO Eastern Department, June 15, 1955.

6. FO/371/120754, "Internal Political Situation in Saudi Arabia" (1956).

7. FO/371/114577, EA1013/10, "Monthly Summary of Events in the Persian Gulf, August 1955"; FO/371/114774, "Labour Situation in Qatar: Strike at QPC" (1955). The strike also brought up the problem of the police force, largely composed of non-Qataris with British officers, and the lack of support it received from the ruler when dealing with Qataris. The attitude of the oil company also came under criticism; apparently minor strikes had occurred every summer since 1951.

8. *Foreign Report*, no. 1233, February 3, 1972. Such demonstrations were distinct from the contemporaneous organized rebellion in Dhufar. The Dhufari rebels, under the banners of PFLOAG and the allied National Democratic Front for the Liberation of Oman and the Arabian Gulf (NDFLOAG) attempted unsuccessfully to extend the rebellion from Dhufar into northern Oman during the early 1970s: a military installation was attacked in June 1970, but all the raiders were captured, and security services were able to make preemptive arrests of other cells in December 1972 and November 1974. Interviews in Oman, 1974–1975.

9. Soliman A. Solaim, "Constitutional and Judicial Organization in Saudi Arabia" (unpublished Ph.D. dissertation, Johns Hopkins University, 1970), 7–39; and Summer Scott Huyette, *Political Adaptation in Sa'udi Arabia: A Study of the Council of Ministers* (Boulder, Colo.: Westview Press, 1985), 53–60. The Con-

sultative Council applied only to the Hijaz because the Hijaz and Najd were regarded as a dual monarchy, similar to Austro-Hungary, until proclamation of the Kingdom of Saudi Arabia in 1932. Even then, the "Basic Instructions" and the council applied only to the Hijaz.

10. Solaim, "Constitutional and Judicial Organization," 77–79.

11. Gerald de Gaury, *Faisal: King of Saudi Arabia* (New York: Frederick A. Praeger, 1966), 147–148.

12. *The Middle East*, no. 13 (November 1975).

13. David Holden and Richard Johns, *The House of Saud: The Rise and Rule of the Most Powerful Dynasty in the Arab World* (New York: Holt, Rinehart, Winston, 1981), 536; *The Middle East*, no. 71 (September 1980): 35.

14. *Sunday Times* (London), December 2, 1984; *Financial Times* (London), April 22, 1985.

15. *Times* (London), March 24, 1987.

16. Interviews in Saudi Arabia.

17. John A. Shaw and David Long, in *Saudi Arabian Modernization: The Impact of Change on Stability* (New York: Praeger, 1982; Washington Paper, no. 89), 86, note that the *majlis* system still exists in Saudi Arabia at the highest levels (comprising the king and leading princes), "but is being slowly eroded by the press of business. At the provincial and local levels, however, it is still the most effective means of communication between governors and governed and is preferred by many Saudis over less-personalized city councils or other representative bodies." They also note that the personal nature of the *majlis* constitutes both a strength and a weakness in the political system: "The greatest political disaffection among the average segment of the population has been in areas where local and provincial amirs have been the least responsive to the people."

18. Emile A. Nakhleh, "Political Participation and the Constitutional Experiments in the Arab Gulf: Bahrain and Qatar," in Tim Niblock, ed., *Social and Economic Development in the Arab Gulf* (London: Croom Helm, for the University of Exeter Centre for Arab Gulf Studies, 1980), 174.

19. Ibid., 175.

20. Text of July 3, 1986 address to the nation, published in *al-Watan*, July 4, 1986 (Foreign Broadcast Information Service, Middle East and Africa, July 7, 1986).

21. Quoted in *Saudi Arabia Newsletter*, May 26, 1986.

Index